BISON
BOOKS

D1040172

2.99

University of Nebraska Press   Lincoln & London

Story of a Montana Childhood

A Short Season

Don Morehead *&* Ann Morehead

© 1998 by the University of Nebraska Press
Manufactured in the United States of America

⊖ The paper in this book meets the minimum requirements of American National Standard for Information Sciences—Permanence of Paper for Printed Library Materials, ANSI z39.48-1984.

Library of Congress
Cataloging-in-Publication Data
Morehead, Donald M.
    A short season : story of a Montana childhood / Don Morehead and Ann Morehead.
    p.   cm.
    ISBN 0-8032-8244-3 (pa : alk. paper)
    1. Cut Bank Region (Mont.)—Biography.
2. Cut Bank Region (Mont.)—Social life and customs.   3. Ranch life—Montana—Cut Bank Region.   4. Blackfeet Indian Reservation (Mont.)—Biography.   5. Morehead, Donald M.—Childhood and youth.   I. Morehead, Ann E.
II. Title.
F739.C77M67   1998
978.6'52—DC21   97-33357
[B]   CIP

In memory of Bill *and* Jack *and* Elizabeth

And for Olive, Donna *and* Joleen, Kerstin *and* Will

Contents

Illustrations

Acknowledgments

Thanks first to Bill Kittredge, who took the time to read an early draft of these pages and pronounce it a book. To Wes Jackson, Allan Bogue, and Robert Swartout Jr., who kindly reviewed the manuscript and offered us their valuable suggestions. And to Lucia Eames, our friend for all seasons, who lent her keen eye and good heart to us whenever we asked.

Thanks also to those who listened to and read pieces of this story as we worked on it: Marvin Johnson, Bob, Teri, and Amanda Averack, Susan and Joe Ray, Sharon Guse, Mary Stolte, Wayne Morehead, Darrell Morehead, Gary Hamer, Ruth Bradley, Don Bradley, Georgia Cornell, Don Cunningham, Ed and Jane Cunningham, Terry and Pat Daugharty, Kenneth DeBey, Llisa Demetrios, Eames Demetrios, Keith Howard, Florence Palmer, Dana Perry, Molly Rife, Lew and Joyce Scheffey, Gary Shepard, Don Van Derby.

Prologue: Getting There

Exiled by death from people we have known,
We are reduced again by years, and try
To call them back and clothe the barren bone,
Not to admit that people ever die.
DONALD HALL

I grew up on a sheep ranch in the middle of the Blackfeet Indian Reservation in Montana. A half century later the ranch is still recognizable but changed by time and economic demands. It is a farm now: Tractors have replaced the horses, and crops grow on the grasslands that once grazed the sheep and before them the buffalo. These days the north range is strip- and block-farmed by Hutterites, who grow wheat, barley, and canola—two seasons on and one off. The dirt path scored with narrow tire tracks has made way for a graded two-lane road; the cable bridge crossing the river below the sheep shed has been replaced by a cement one. Years ago, the shed burned and was never rebuilt. The bunkhouse, moved up the road somehow, now sleeps seasonal farmhands at its new site. The garage and the granary crumble from age.

For seven years, my family lived on this land that is measured in miles rather than acres. My older sister took part in many of the experiences I relate here, but her memories have taken a shape different from mine. Born after the family came to the ranch and barely five when my father died, my younger sister remembers almost nothing from that time. Even in the early days of her grief, when she most keenly missed her husband, my mother didn't regret leaving the hard work and isolation of ranch life. After we moved to town and she remarried, she folded up the past and put it away as carefully as she did the family keepsakes.

None of us has lived in Montana for fifty years now. Dad is buried in the cemetery that runs along the Santa Rita Road north of Cut Bank. What I have left of him is a scattering of artifacts, salvaged pieces of a way of life that do little to bring back my memory of him: a pair of sheep shears hanging in the basement of my city house, a jackknife, a Hamilton pocket watch, the brass face of a Chatillon wool scale. The .20-gauge shotgun my father used when he hunted ducks is propped in one corner of a closet, and a sheep bell, the patella of a yearling hanging by rawhide for a clangor, sits on a bookshelf.

Inside a leather Western Life Insurance pouch, envelopes separate tax records, life insurance policies, and loans at the Great Falls National Bank from the single remaining sheet of his stationery, frayed and discolored now. He designed the logo himself: an unfurled ribbon stretches between a ewe and an oil well, a ram's head between them. Dad's name and PO box number are printed below. The reverse side is a Blackfeet reservation map with the location of the ranch starred at its center. The flyleaves of a *Farmer's Year Book* give land measures, parcel post rates, interest tables, and remedies for animal diseases. Inside, advances against the herders' wages and the count for the four bands of sheep my father ran in 1945 and 1946 are carefully recorded in a single hand. The last note he wrote turned up in a trunk the foreman kept at the foot of his bed. There are no letters.

I have a few early snapshots of my father with the packhorses that he used to tend the Forest Service camps above Heart Butte. Even these photographs do not convey much of a feeling for our way of life then, or of Dad. Looking at them, I feel only a blurred sense of recognition of the muscles and lines in his face, the strong veins in his hands. In the custom of the times, he wore a hat, and his face is often shadowed by it. In his wedding picture he looks almost a caricature of himself, younger and more citified than my memory of him, familiar because my mother is sitting beside him.

Dad at a U.S. Forest Service camp in 1933

After we moved to the ranch in 1941, the photographs we took skip across the years. The big ice flood on the river after World War II takes up several pages in a wood-backed album. In one snapshot, my father stands proudly in front of the new cab-over truck; my airplane car is parked nearby, axle-deep in snow. He wears an army sweater and wide suspenders buttoned to his denim pants. In another photo, my sister poses on her horse in front of the sheep shed. I sit proudly in the metal cab of the jeep pulling myself forward with the steering wheel so I can reach the pedals. My mother appears here and there in the album, standing in the yard, sometimes with my younger sister, but most often when there is a gathering of her family. Most of the time, she was behind the camera.

Like these photographs, my childhood memories emerge a frame or two at a time, shaped and stored in muffled pieces—dreams almost—upstaged always by the sorrow I felt when my father died just before my childhood ended. This sadness, which can still overwhelm me, pushes back my recollections of what was wonderful then, hiding my wordless images of him and our short season together.

I unearthed my father's world when I danced along in the rhythms of his actions, read his emotions the way I read the currents in the river where I fished. Even now when I search for the image of his face, try to hear the resonance of his voice or to visualize his long stride, I realize that I must settle for remembering those things we did together. Happily, my child memory recorded much of the seven years we lived on the ranch where I had everything a boy ever wanted—a horse, a *BB* gun, a fishing pole, a real army jeep to drive, and my dad. Bits of that world have remained alive in the stories I've told and retold my own children about our life then—narratives about tending camp and shearing and haying, tales of mad herders and rampaging bears, long-day summers and forever winters.

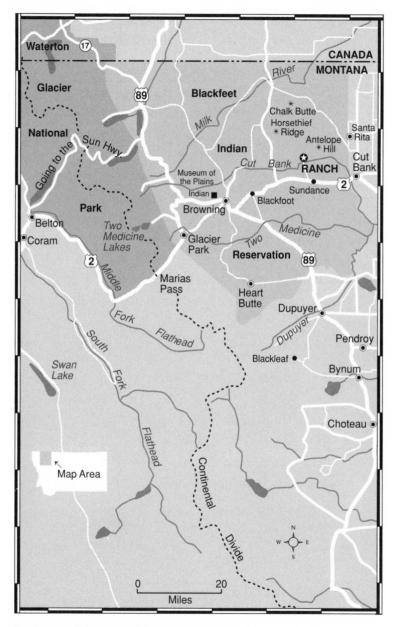

Region around the ranch, 1942. *Map by Ellen McElhinny*

Backgrounds

Once in his life a man ought to concentrate his mind upon the remembered earth, I believe. He ought to give himself up to a particular landscape in his experience, to look at it from as many angles as he can, to wonder about it, to dwell upon it. He ought to imagine that he touches it with his hands at every season and listens to the sounds that are made upon it. He ought to imagine the creatures there and all the faintest motions of the wind. He ought to recollect the glare of noon and all the colors of dawn and dusk.—N. SCOTT MOMADAY

Beginnings

The fertile mountain valleys in western Montana attracted migrants as early as the 1840s, the mining camps near Butte and Helena a decade or two later. In 1877 the Desert Land Act, along with the Homestead Acts and renegotiated Indian treaties, opened large sections of land for white settlements. By the time my father was born in 1911, railroads like the Great Northern had crisscrossed the territory and were aggressively promoting bargain fares to cheap land on the central and eastern plains. Early homesteaders arrived there to claim first a pitiful 160 acres, and later, stakes double that size but still inadequate to support a family in dry years—even with Campbell's new methods of dryland farming. Along with 115,000 other settlers, all four of my grandparents came west around the turn of the century to seek their fortunes in the Treasure State. Even if their lives were no better for it, opportunity, a clear sense of purpose, and a piece of land were what mattered to them.

Both of my parents were raised south of the Blackfeet reservation, my father at Bynum and my mother first at Farmington and then at Choteau. My father's family arrived in Montana at the turn of the century. His father, Asher Bright Morehead, came from Lancaster, Missouri, and his mother, Mary Schwartz, from Buffalo, New York. After serving in the Spanish American War, Asher was a hunting guide and scout for parties that included Teddy Roosevelt. In 1909 he met Mary at the newly built Graves Hotel in Harlowton, where he had opened the town's first barbershop and she cooked in the hotel kitchen.

But my grandfather had always dreamed of owning his own spread, and soon after they were married, they took title to their first 160 acres on the American River out of Harlowton, where both my father, William Asher, and his younger sister, Esther, were born. As soon as their first homestead was titled, after a five-year prove-up period, the family sold and moved again, first to Billings and Fort Benton and then to homestead land near Blackleaf Canyon, west of Bynum, that was available under the Enlarged Homestead Act. My father's younger brother, Dubs, was born at Billings in 1916.

The family survived the dry years on the steady income my grandmother brought in from her town job. Every Sunday night she rode the bus to Great Falls, where she worked for six days in the Rainbow Hotel, returning each Saturday after work for a single day at home with her family. My grandfather was a horse trader and a bootlegger whose solution to hard times was an enterprising if sometimes makeshift self-reliance. He kept a herd of livestock and a flock of chicks, planted a big garden each summer, dug an elaborate root cellar where he stored potatoes and hung onions, turnips, and beets, put up some hay to sell, and, of course, traded horses and sold booze. Good-natured, gregarious, and easy-going, he enjoyed people, maintaining friendships that lasted his lifetime.

In contrast, my grandmother was a stern and nervous woman who put duty above even family life. She was brought up to work, like most of the women who came west to make their lives. Spared an early death in childbirth, by her mid-fifties she had become a spent and broken soul, left alone by the death of her husband and the marriages of her children. After a minor gall bladder operation in the spring of 1937, she became disoriented and depressed; that fall she collapsed and died from a cerebral hemorrhage. I never met either of my paternal grandparents. Asher died in 1932, Mary a few months before I was born.

I did know my mother's parents, Dewitt and Cynthia Seekins,

who left New York to homestead in Canada at the turn of the century. Fleeing the harsh winters in Elbow, Saskatchewan, they crossed the border in 1914 and resettled in Sunburst, Montana, attracted perhaps as much by the name of the place as by the newly available land-settlement grants. Arriving with four children, they found the conditions in Montana not very different from those they had left behind.

Still, they set about making a life at dryland farming, and my grandfather worked as a mechanic in town to buy what they didn't make or grow. In Montana, they produced four more children—my mother, Olive, two other daughters, and their only son. The son and two daughters died in early childhood. Having satisfied the five-year title requirement, they sold and moved the family in 1920 to Farmington and then again to Choteau, where my grandfather managed grain elevators and for the first time could depend on a steady outside income to support his five girls.

My maternal grandmother was a taciturn woman whose disaffection with frontier life was reflected in her long-suffering expression. Kids seemed a bother to her even though she had had eight of her own, losing a boy and two girls along the way. As children, my mother and aunts tried not to ask my grandmother questions because she would consult her "reference books" and force them to endure lengthy tutorials. During her eighth pregnancy, she fell down a flight of stairs and injured her back. From that time on, she walked bent over at the waist, and in later years required a cane.

The places my maternal grandparents lived always reminded me of the cottage rooms I had seen pictured in *The Saturday Evening Post*. Antimacassars were pinned to the arms and backs of the overstuffed furniture; framed pictures and figurines cluttered doily-covered table tops. They had no plumbing except running water; a chamber pot sat next to each bed most of the fall and all through the winter. My grandmother read or knitted while she sat in her rocking chair, waving a fan in front of her sweating face when it was cool outside, wrapping herself in a shawl because she had felt a chill in summer heat.

My grandfather spent his life working at just average jobs—doing auto repairs in a garage, tending elevators and oil fields, running a grocery store in Pendroy—but he carried himself in a way that suggested time and opportunity had not afforded him his due. In spite of his commonplace jobs, he seldom wore a working man's clothes but dressed instead in wool pants and dress coats, the ill-fitting sleeves of his dress shirts tailored by elastic elbow bands that evened the cuffs at the wrists. His high-topped black shoes laced to the ankle, and garters wrapped below his knees held up his socks. He helped my grandmother do the heavy work around the house and he took delight in cooking Sunday supper. His favorite: creamed asparagus on toast.

Dewitt Seekins, or "Guy," as he liked to be called, spoke often, at times passionately, about the conditions of the common man and the need to help anyone who had fallen on hard times. After fifteen years homesteading in one of the continent's most hostile climates, he understood that success depended more on weather than on character.

My own parents met the year after my mother graduated from high school, when the two of them were working on a ranch near Dupuyer—he as a hand and she as a cook's helper. My mother was attracted to my father's good looks, his optimism and confidence, but initially she was put off by his willingness to forgo convention and even defy the established social order. He drank and fought too much, she and her family thought. My father was one of the Bynum boys, a fraternal group who seldom missed a chance after work to get together, who loved drinking and dancing at the Saturday night dances up the side stairs above the saloon that served as their clubhouse.

After my parents married in the fall of 1934, they hired on as a working couple on the ranch of Johnny Sullivan. Again, Mother helped to cook and clean, but Dad was now in charge of a ranch crew. Both my older sister, Donna, and I were born during their stay there, my sister in the fall of 1936 and I a year later. My mother was exhausted by her consecutive pregnancies and more than a little unhappy with her role as maid to the teenaged Sullivan children. When she packed up my sister and me and left for a brief but convincing stay with her parents, my father started to look around in earnest for a place to run on shares where he could put together his first herd of cattle.

Up on the Blackfeet reservation, Angeline Connelly had such a place on land lease. There my father could run his cows in exchange for taking care of the Connelly herd and split the proceeds from the hay crop he would put up. My parents had been there only a year when a better opportunity arose. Johnny Sullivan's son, Emmett, had hurt his back and was putting his ranch up for shares. In the fall of 1939, Dad sold his cattle and moved back to Dupuyer, where he bought his first band of ewes to lamb in the spring. After two lambings, he had built up the band to about fifteen hundred sheep, always keeping in mind the settler's game plan—start with livestock but end with land.

In the most telling photograph from these early years, my parents stand on either side of a giant homemade "STOP" sign set up to mark entry to a mountain sheep camp, appropriately named "Palookaville." The sign details the demographics of the place. The altitude is listed as "Higher 'n Hell," and the population "one more since you came." It also publishes the laws. The speed limit is

My parents at a sheep camp, August 1937

"slow"; "Horses, dogs, and camp idiots" are to have the "right away." One W. A. Morehead—my father—is named as "Justice of the Peace." Dad, his hat tilted at a jaunty angle that shadows his eyes but reveals a puckish grin, relaxes against his side of the sign. On the opposite side, my mother stands rigid and stares woodenly away from the camera. She is seven months pregnant with me. I suspect this photo captures the spirit of their early marriage.

By 1941, World War II had created a sudden increase in the demand for both meat and wool. A few years earlier, a shrewd Frenchman named Art Pardue had bought a ranch between Browning and Cut Bank, taken grazing leases on Blackfeet reservation land, and was running several bands of sheep there. Now, he wanted to capitalize on the war demand by increasing his flock and securing more leases on the reservation. When Pardue invited Dad to become his "split half" partner in the summer of 1941, it was just the opportunity my father had been looking for. He eagerly accepted, and he and my mother packed up the few pieces of furniture they had accumulated and a new Maytag washer driven by a gasoline motor and trailed their motley band of crossed Cotswolds, Columbians, Hampshires, and Rambouillets to the reservation ranch that fall.

Early in 1942, less than six months after we had settled in at the ranch, my father got his notice to report for military duty. When he went to the draft board to ask for a little time to dispose of the sheep and relocate his family, the board agreed to review his status. Weeks later, my father was notified that he had been reclassified because of his critical occupation. Although he was happy that he wouldn't be forced to sell out, my father still had mixed feelings about not being an active participant in the war, and this ambivalence never left him in the following years. My mother was simply relieved. All the young men who had come from Dupuyer to work for Dad had signed up after the attack on Pearl Harbor. His brother Dubs had already been shipped out to the Philippines and on May 5, 1942, he was captured by the Japanese on the island of Corregidor. Before the war ended, he would spend three and half years in Japanese prisoner of war camps, a survivor of the Bataan March.

Both my parents were exhilarated by what they saw as their big chance to make it, but in their early days on the ranch, each reacted differently to its demands. With three older sisters at home, my mother hadn't learned much about housekeeping, including how to start a fire in a stove or how to cook on one. A mixed bundle of grit and softness, she was so willing to pitch in that at first she accepted any assignment whether or not she was suited for it or had the skills to carry it out. On a ranch there is always more work than can be done, and my father was quick to include her as his partner, asking her to drive the truck while he unloaded oil cake, to help remove a birthing lamb since her hands were small enough for the job. He called her "little fellow" rather than Olive, preferring the nickname he affectionately coined on their wedding night when he saw her tiny feet.

But even in her excitement with the new ranch, my mother was soon overwhelmed by the demands of caring for two young children, cooking for ranch hands as well as the family, and keeping house with primitive equipment. She signaled her growing distress to my father in a variety of indirect ways, fainting from exhaustion, crying too quickly. By the spring of 1942, my father understood that she had reached her limits and hired household help. About the same time, he also found Jimmy Dunbar, a jockey-sized man of mixed Irish-Indian ancestry, who stayed on as his trusted hand.

The constant demands and hard work of the ranch suited my father better. He reveled in running his own operation and easily carried the responsibilities that went with it. Always on the move, he seldom walked at a normal pace and I found myself running alongside him to keep up. He was both high spirited and even tempered; any anger he showed came on suddenly and lifted in its own good time. His beliefs, untempered by higher education, had sharp boundaries although he was generally tolerant of a first fall from grace. I remember occasions when he was harsh with adults, always demanding of those who worked with him, but toward my sisters and me he was protective, indulgent even, and I am still surprised when a favorite aunt says he was often too hard on me. Certainly, he was the driving force and inspiration in our lives, the hub around which activity spun. As a young boy, I was drawn into that whirl of energy, and by the time I was six, I had become his small partner. Except for the time I spent in school and playing with my sisters, I was at his side for the next five years.

The Ranch

The Rocky Mountains are an enormous slab of Precambrian belt rock formed by thrusting faults into jagged peaks separated from one another by deep valleys ice age glaciers carved. These stone titans tracked the western edge of the reservation. Framing the lower horizon, their profiles anchored those of us who lived on the plains. Even the names of these peaks—Big Chief, Rising Wolf, White Calf—suggest an intimate history, a private connection with those below who depend on their permanence. Whenever we looked west, we saw our mountains. When we left for longer than a week, or it was overcast for days together, their absence was what we felt first.

Stretched below the jutting peaks of the Rockies, the rich grazing lands on the western half of the Blackfeet Indian Reservation and the large federal tracts bordering Glacier National Park make ideal sheep country. Gentle hills mold the land where flat-topped, rock-bordered buttes rise off the plains like giant altars. Long before white settlers came, the Blackfeet, without horses or guns, found in these natural ledges—or *piskans,* as they called them— perfect stages from which to stampede the buffalo. Sweeping between the buttes lie ancient glacial lake beds, their borders outlined by steep ridges. These glacial beds grow the thick bunch and buffalo grasses that grazed the sheep and the migrating herds of elk, antelope, and buffalo before them.

All day, often well into the night, the west wind blows with authority. Even in its gentler aspects it rolls the grass in waves across the plains, turning willow and cottonwood leaves from green to quicksilver and pulling clouds apart like taffy. In late summer, a single gust can shatter a haystack or lift a roof into the sky like a giant wooden kite. Through the long months of winter, cattle push against its howling blizzard fury while sheep huddle, unable even to graze. We struggled against this natural vengeance, corralled our animals and battened down our buildings, but as a child I played with the wind, shouldering against it, letting it carry me along, a boy prairie schooner.

Above the plains, the Montana sky is always in motion, with wind-strewn clouds streaking across its surface. Reading its lines, people can work out daily clues to the volatile weather. At night the northern lights flare like streamers at the edge of the horizon. Unlike the mountains, black backdrops in darkness, the sky is always alive. It was a heavenly spectacle for us as we looked up, lying on the ground like Bedouin children.

The Blackfeet Indian Reservation begins at the bridge that crosses the Cut Bank River on the edge of the town of the same name and extends west toward Glacier National Park and the Rocky Mountains. For twenty miles or so, small farms and ranches, remnants of the agricultural programs developed for the Indians during the 1920s, dot the landscape in a patchwork of hay fields and strip-farm plantings of wheat, barley, and yellow mustard. A few miles east of Blackfoot, a railroad stop halfway to Browning, the grasslands that stretch beyond the Canadian border begin. Four miles north of Highway 2 along the Cut Bank River, at the end of a dirt road, was our ranch—twenty-five hundred acres with another eight thousand of north range, some leased from the Blackfeet tribe.

At the top of the bluff that looked down on the ranch, a small grave was enclosed by a weary picket fence. A barely legible wooden marker for a small child, perhaps its mother as well, stood at one end of it, with a few large stones around its base for support. As children playing there, we never did decipher the name on the

Mother and Dad with Joleen in front of the ranch house, 1947

marker and nobody seemed to know who the grave belonged to or exactly how long it had been there. During the summer when the river was low, my sister and I would cross on our horses at the end of the bluff and ride up to the grave. But we rarely ventured inside the fence in our superstitious fears that we might step on the bodies buried there.

From the bluff, we could look down on the six ranch buildings clustered along the river below. Seen from above, three of these structures—our house, a cookhouse where the seasonal work crews ate, and a bunkhouse—formed the points of a triangle. The Cut Bank River flowed directly below the bluff past the house and the big sheep shed. Beyond the three houses, a long hill ran parallel to the river. Tunneled into the side of the hill like an Idaho potato cellar were a deep garage and a granary, its cement stalls full of oil cake for the sheep and oats for the horses. Everything we left outside—stacks of corral panels and steel stakes, posts and fencing wire, haying machinery, and odd piles of lumber and metal parts— was stored on the crown of the hill. Our dump was located in a small coulee at the far end of it, but in reality we never threw much away. Recycling meant fewer trips to town.

Down from the house, next to the river, the gray-and-red sheep shed with its pitched roof and two side wings was the first building to pull the eye when you looked down from the bluff above. Each year we had to clean manure out of the main section and horse stalls with a stone boat, a big iron tub open at one end with a handle to tip it once it was pulled outside by our strongest team.

One side wing parallel to the main section was divided into mangers where we fed the work horses we used for haying; their leather harnesses and thick collars hung on the wall nearby. These were good harnesses with ivory terrets to guide the reins and chromed tips for the oak horns attached to the neck collars. The halters and bridles for our Shetland pony and a black quarter horse named Tony hung low on wooden pegs where my sister and I could reach them. We seldom rode with saddles, nor did the older Indian boys who arrived unannounced during the summer months to swim with us in the river and play in the shed.

The other wing of the sheep shed was divided into stalls along one wall for the individual sheep shearers who arrived in May like a touring summer carnival troupe. It was one of the few times during the year when there were people on the ranch besides the family and a hired hand or two. Sheep ranching is a lonely business, and the shearers, the wool tiers, and the stompers were a mixed crew of interesting characters, some bringing wives and children who became company and playmates for my mother and my two sisters and me. Exciting activity, friends during the day, and baseball games at night made shearing the best time of year.

My father designed the sheep shed and oversaw its construction in 1943, the second spring we lived on the ranch. The old one had burned down the winter before. He was particularly proud of his handiwork, and even before its completion he had been keeping his eye out for just the right contrasting colors to paint it. Traveling down to the Klamath Valley in Oregon that spring to buy lambs, he came up over a rise that looked down on a picturesque spread in the valley below. The buildings there were painted a light steel gray and trimmed in barn red. He was so taken by the look of the place that he stopped by town the afternoon he got back and picked up a sprayer so he could paint the sheep shed and all the other outbuildings in the same color scheme.

The ranch house was constructed of lodgepole pine logs with gray cement mortar plugging the gaps between them. Sometime before we came to live there, this structure had been stuccoed over and painted, and an L-shaped porch and pantry off the kitchen had been added on. The upper half of the porch was screened so we could sit outside on summer nights without being pestered by the huge mosquitoes that multiplied in the stale water flooding above river banks. From the porch, we could see the river making its way through the basin below the bluffs and the swallows swirling in front of the shed. Around the back of the house a weather break of graduated trees protected us from blizzard drifts in winter and the hot west summer winds. It was also a place where each of us lost favorite toys.

There were three bedrooms on the main floor, one behind the kitchen for the housekeeper, and two for the family at the end of the long combination living-dining area. Along with the cookstove, a large kerosene stove heated the house. It stood in the area where we ate our family meals and relaxed at night while my mother crocheted and Dad listened for war news and the livestock report. Upstairs, my sisters and I played hide-and-seek when it was too late or too cold to play outside, setting up miniature houses with sheets and blankets next to the large enclosed storage areas under the eaves.

Our place was the only one on that part of the reservation with a wind charger for electric lights and a reserve tank in the attic for cold water to flush a toilet and fill a bath. Neighboring ranchers and Indian families still burned kerosene lanterns and used out-houses, hand pumps, and tin tubs. When they stopped by, they were generally curious about the technical intricacies of our wind charger and pump, eager to give our toilet a flush and flip the electric wall switches on and off.

In the basement, large glass batteries stored the electricity generated by the wind charger, lining almost an entire wall. We used copper pennies to make burnt fuses work again. In the same room, ceiling-high shelves held much of the food stored for the winter months, when getting into town for supplies was difficult. Glass jars with rubber-sealed lids held canned beef, corn, carrots, peas, string beans, strawberry preserves, peaches, cherries, pears, and sliced sweet pickles.

We raised or grew part of the food we ate, and throughout the summer my mother canned for days at a time in an ongoing sweet-smelling ritual that she said reminded her of home. After my father plowed and harrowed the soil each spring with a team of horses, he and my mother would plant an early summer garden—bigger during the war than after. During summer days, my sisters and I would open the gate to the garden and look for garter snakes and rabbits between the rows of lettuces, radishes, beans, potatoes, beets, and carrots. On our way out we would stop to pull a few baby carrots, wiping them on our shirt tails before we ate them.

Near the cellar door stood an Easy washer with separate wash and spin tubs. My mother had been more than a little pleased to replace her old wringer-style washer with one that also rinsed and spun the clothes damp dry in one operation. All kinds of household supplies and boxes of fresh food were stored on an elevated wood floor in the cellar to keep them dry. Here were slatted wooden baskets, flat-lidded and tapered, filled with apples individually wrapped in dark-purple tissue paper, and boxes of oranges layered in gray cardboard embossed to fit their shape. The heavy door to the basement was always left open during the summer, and we would tromp down the wide, wooden steps to munch an apple or get an orange for Mother to peel. Unwrapping the crinkly paper from an apple is a pleasure I still miss.

Over the door of the woodshed next to the house, Dad wired a buffalo skull—a favorite pediment for outbuildings and gates on ranches. My sister Donna and I had found it exposed in the cutbank of the river one summer when the water was low. On warm days, we used the outside privy next to the woodshed to save water. The slick pages of a Sears and Roebuck catalog piled inside next to the heart-shaped hole in the wood seat was nearly useless as toilet paper. If either Donna or I entered for a private moment when my father was around, he would rock this little structure, but the privy was bulky enough that our efforts to play the same joke on him went almost unnoticed.

An old-style dinner bell the size of a wash bucket hung on a log post just outside the back door of the pantry. My sister and I raced to be first to call the men to dinner. The loser would wait until the rich tone faded between bluff and hills, then ring the bell again. Impatient if the second ring failed, my mother would then send one of us out to fetch them.

The bunkhouse and cookhouse, two nearly square, stuccoed buildings with pitched roofs where summer swallows nested in the eaves, looked like mill houses built in the 1920s on the Indian land-grant farms nearby. The smaller one was the cookhouse. There all of us, even my mother and the household help, ate at long tables during shearing and haying. My father hired ex-military and hotel cooks for the season. One retired navy cook, I recall, was so efficient he always had the lunch dishes washed and was standing with one foot on the panel to watch the shearers before the last man had finished eating.

These professionals served food we had never tasted before, exotic dishes like lasagne and quiche, but it is their pies I remember with a longing never satisfied by the pale counterparts I order now in restaurants. In a dazzling if unpredictable variety—peach, banana, apple, coconut cream, rhubarb, cherry, raspberry, blueberry, custard—they always appeared as part of the fare, the quality of the crust separating the great from the merely delicious.

My father's foreman, Jimmy Dunbar, and the hired hands lived in the bunkhouse, a single room with a potbellied stove in the center, its long pipe extending into the chimney on the roof. Three beds and a cot or two, each with a chest or footlocker, sometimes an old suitcase at its foot, marked out the perimeter into separate territories. Near the front door stood a sink with a speckled gray enamel basin, and soiled, dark-colored towels hung on nails next to the cloudy mirror above it. The men who washed up here always went through the same motions, first washing their hands, then lifting discolored water out of the pan to splash it over their faces and across the backs of their necks with a few quick rubs. After toweling off, they would swirl the water in the basin and toss it outside. Donna and I seldom entered the bunkhouse unless Jimmy was there. The place smelled like dirty pillows, and after one of the night herders invited us to "play nasty," it became the only place on the ranch where we didn't feel comfortable.

After my father had painted the sheep shed and gone on with his new sprayer to match up the other buildings, the two of us drove up to the bluff late one afternoon to get a bird's eye view of his artistry. He was never much one for self-congratulation, but on this occasion his grin was smug enough to betray his satisfaction with the choice of colors, and more than that, his pride at having arrived at this plateau of opportunity. No matter that our place didn't look as idyllic as the spread he had caught sight of in the sheltered Klamath Valley, with its stands of mature trees and picturesque meandering streams; the paint had given the ranch a cohesive appearance, an aura of structure and order.

And I can still see, as clearly as if I were standing there now, looking down in that moment just before he turned back to the jeep and nodded at me to hurry along, all of that little world below—the cluster of newly painted outbuildings where the men were finishing up the day's work, all bright in the afternoon sun, the river moving along below them, the grasslands where the sheep grazed stretching out beyond the gate. This was my paradise for seven years. Calling it to mind now is as easy as it was to take it all in then, to record it carefully, detail by detail, in the unselfconscious joy of my childhood.

The River

The Cut Bank River rises near Pitamakan Pass, below Mount Morgan in Glacier National Park. Like the mountains, it offers those who live on its banks a steady companionship as well as a running commentary on the cycles and seasons. Flowing thirty to fifty feet wide in gentle S curves as it passes the ranch, it makes its way to meet the Two Medicine and become the Marias before it merges with the Missouri. The bluestem grass on either side of the river is taller and more dense than the short bunch and buffalo grasses out on the north range, and it is home to many of the rabbits, weasels, minks, beavers, muskrats, porcupines, and snakes that live along the banks.

Late in the spring, the beavers cut the birches and willows that grow along the river to repair their dams and houses from the ravages of winter ice and mountain runoff. Their cousins, the muskrats, live up the steep banks in narrow tunnels hidden by chokecherry and gooseberry bushes. In early summer, the receding river supplies the mud the swallows need to build their nests and opens access to fishermen and swimmers along its banks. Honkers and ducks fleeing the early autumn frosts farther north stop over in their migration about the time the rabbits' fur turns white. My father hunted both. When icy edges narrowed the river, a mink occasionally ventured away from the banks to sneak into the henhouse for a meal; otherwise we rarely knew they were there.

As a child, I became attached to the river and its meadows much the way the chicks my father bought in flats like strawberries imprinted on those of us who tended them. I fished and swam in it and studied its currents—the sudden ripples over gravel beds, the fast shallow water, the quieter-moving deep, blue bends. In the heat of summer evenings, I chewed stems of timothy grass and watched dragonflies and stoneflies and mayflies perform their ballet above the slow water; flying ants and spruce bugs and mosquitoes swarmed and hovered along the banks.

Of all the animals that lived on the river, the beavers were the most reclusive. In the early evening, we would walk down to watch them work. During the spring and summer they repaired their dams and houses, anchoring the twig mounds on the banks of the island directly across from the sheep shed. On the island they found plenty of bark and foliage, and they and their young ones were protected there from the menace of ranch dogs. Even in the stillest water, the beavers made barely noticeable wakes, their shiny, otterlike heads moving along just above the surface as they went about their earnest business. We seldom saw a beaver leave the water to begin its swagger up the island bank with its broad, flat tail slapping along behind it.

The shiny pelts of the smaller muskrats were easy to spot as they swam along the bank where they burrowed homes. Active most of the day, they fed on the grasses and the chokecherry, gooseberry, and black currant bushes that lined the river, and when I fished there in the summer months, one often scurried into the water ahead of me. Once in the water, the muskrat would move along quickly through the current, propelling itself with jerking thrusts of its partially webbed feet in front of a wake of tiny bobbing waves.

All through the fall, my father hunted Canadian mallards and geese, blue- and green-winged teal, and canvasbacks on their way south from the wheat and barley fields in Canada. He seldom invited me to go along. With nothing but clustered chokecherry bushes and willows to hide his progress along the bank, surprising a flock of birds floating midstream was tricky enough without a child in tow. Even alone, he was not always successful; his single-

Cut Bank River at the end of a spring thaw

shot .20-gauge was more suited to swallows and rabbits than ducks and geese.

In the winter the river froze over and became a place of beauty, but it was treacherous to those who trusted it. Most mornings during a cold spell, my father went down to re-open holes along the banks so the sheep and horses could drink. Later in the day I would venture down to test the strength of the ice for skating and sledding. Leaning back on one foot as I stepped off the bank, I would inch forward across the snow-dusted ice holding my breath. The sharp crack I dreaded signaled a drop into a foot of frigid water. Bruising my shins through icy wet trousers, I would break my way to shore, using my elbows as hammers.

In early spring, chinook winds broke the solid surface into huge ice blocks that pushed along in the sluggish current, crashing and screeching against one another, sometimes threatening to sweep away the cable bridge. Later in the season, high water from the melting snow in the mountains spilled over the banks, then receded as gradually as it appeared.

My most vivid memories of a forbidding river date from the late spring when my three-year-old sister, Joleen, broke her arm. We had been all but stranded on the ranch by high water, with only the back road that led to the highway southwest of Santa Rita open for escapes. To get my sister to a doctor without bumping her up and down in the truck (we had no telephone or radio for emergencies), my father drove along the river as far as the nearest ranch on the opposite bank and honked the horn until a neighbor came outside. Dad yelled across, asking him to drive to town and charter a plane to pick us up, the kind of bold solution he often favored.

A few hours later, a small plane landed in an open area at the river bend below the cable bridge. It was a four-passenger craft, two seats in back and two in front. My older sister, Donna, and I stood a little to the side watching, worried that we might not be included in this excitement. After he had climbed into the back seat with Joleen, Dad called, "Come on, you kids; you can have your first plane ride."

Donna crawled into the back seat to hold Joleen's legs, and I scrambled into the front with the pilot. I do not remember much about the flight—nothing at all of the takeoff or the landing—but as we rose up over the swollen river, I looked out to see the neighboring fields fall away beyond the window and suddenly realized where I was relative to the ground. For the remainder of the short trip, I fixed my attention on the moving needles of the instrument panel.

Two bridges crossed the river on our property. We used the cable bridge below the sheep shed unless the river was flooded in the spring or stressed with ice during the winter. This span was so narrow my father would hang his head out the window when he drove across to keep the tire tracked to the very edge. The second bridge, a submerged cement slab, lay upstream toward the old Monroe place. Useless in ice or high water, it served large trucks hauling feed or wool throughout the summer and delivering lambs in the fall. Getting across the river in different vehicles, with livestock or machinery, was nearly always an ordeal for the adults, but for me it offered a carnival ride of excitement.

When we were forced to cross away from the bridges, Dad disconnected the fan belt on the jeep before easing it into the river. With no fan blades to whip water over the engine and short it out, the motor continued to run. As long as the headlights were above water, we could make the crossing, with waves rolling and pushing against the wide radiator grille and the fender wells. Even with the jeep's low center of gravity, we didn't worry if the floorboards in the cab were flooded as long as the wiring and our canvas seats stayed dry. Once across, the jeep's four-wheel drive easily pulled us over the slippery rocks and up the muddy banks.

All through the summer we would ford work and riding horses, dogs and sheep across the river. The work horses were usually compliant about dragging mowers, rakes, and wagons to the other side for July haying. Still, some horses, sensing the hard pull through the water and the climb up the rutted bank, resisted fording the river even when it was low. If one of the horses in a team refused to wade in, my father would get off the mower or rake and ride the animal across, encouraging each step with a tap from a freshly cut willow whip.

When the river was low, Donna and I would ride our horses to favorite places up and down its banks. Near the ranch, we looked for easy crossings, spots where the fast water ran shallow next to gravel bars and we could ford knee deep on Tony and belly high on the Shetland. Farther afield, where the river was less familiar, we were more likely to push our own limits and those of the horses, on occasion overcoming our mounts' reluctance with a few slaps of the leather rein. Sometimes, having reached the swirling blue just past midstream, the horse with only its head above water began to bob. I would grab for the longer hairs of the mane and grip the reins to keep from being washed off in the jolting shift from wading to swimming. It was always a struggle for the horse to find a place to clamber up the opposite bank after one of these deep swims. Finally safe on the other side, the horse had to be given time to shake itself off before it could be coaxed to move on. For a while, then, until the memory of the last sudden, involuntary swim had faded, I would avoid crossings in areas I didn't know.

My father taught me to fish early, taking me along with him from the time I was six, and we fished the river for rainbow and cutthroat trout in all seasons except winter, when the river was icebound. I learned quickly to set the hook in the instant after a solid strike, but only after Dad had set me up with a wind-up reel that reversed itself with a flick of the lever could I consistently pull in my catch.

When I was eight or nine and could fish by myself, I hung grasshoppers caught after several misses in my cupped hand on #10 Eagle Claw hooks. I dropped my line along the banks, where four feet down clumps of long grass shimmied in the water, and waited for the line to tense. Goldeyes—scavenger fish with sucker mouths and mushy flesh—were easy to hook. I was convinced the goldeyes were taking over the river, so I threw these catches up on the bank for the hawks to eat.

Both large rainbow trout and plump suckers lay on the bottom under the cable bridge. I spent many afternoons alone there, drifting my bait along in downstream currents, where it slipped and skittered over the mud and rocks. The mouths of the fish opened and closed but always spat out my bait before I could flick the tip of the pole just enough to set the hook. Once in a while I would enlist a seasoned fisherman—my uncle, perhaps, or Art Pardue—to help me snare these sluggish giants, but none of us ever caught a single fish under the cable bridge.

Early on my father had waterproofed us, at first letting us paddle in the shallows, finally teaching us to swim in the deepest water. In the hottest afternoons of August, when the fish stopped biting, Donna and I swam in the river, sometimes with our Indian friends, Tim and Frankie. The boys would simply show up on horseback late in the morning, play for a couple of hours, and disappear without a word midafternoon. When I asked Dad why they were so quiet, he told me that they still followed "Indian ways." My sister and I were with the boys the day we found the buffalo head stuck in the river bank.

The four of us had started across the river but had been pulled downstream in the heavy current before we reached our destination on the other side, a spot where the bank was so overgrown we had to pull ourselves along hand over hand. As we were struggling through the thicket of brush to find a clearing, we spotted the skull—it looked like a longhorn steer—embedded in the bank. After digging around the base of it, we freed up the underside from the mud suction holding it in place and gently lifted it out by its horns. We held the skull in the water until it had been rinsed clean. Then we carried it proudly across the bridge and back to the house. My father identified our find as a buffalo skull, and while the four of us gathered around the base of his ladder, he ceremonially wired our trophy above the woodshed door.

Life Cycles

Life flows in metrical rhythms on a Montana ranch, where work is synchronized to the cadences of seasons and cycles of life. Moving along to predictable tempos, we participated in each season, each cycle, and, even as we strained against the elements, found reassuring connections between the natural world and our human one. Standing apart from wilder creatures, we watched and sometimes interfered with their struggles for survival. Over those we had tamed, we held complete sway. But once in a while nature reclaimed power over us, compelling us to concede in a moment of humility.

Late in the spring, when mountain runoff no longer swelled the river and a channel of mud caked the exposed banks, the swallows returned to the ranch. One May morning, a few birds would appear, darting from the mud flats exposed by the receding waters to the wide eaves and gables of the sheep shed. Within days, swarms of little red-brown workers with white striped heads would be frantically scooping mud into their mouths to build their nests. Their wings flapped as if to begin flight as they lifted tiny chunks of mud to shape into balls for their miniature bricks. Midflight between river and nest, they would dive to pluck up stems of dried grass or string to reinforce their curved walls of mud. Crafted as hollow spheres with small, tapered openings for entry, the nests tilted against the upper walls, each other, and the sides of the eaves. This sturdy architectural design sheltered first eggs, then newly hatched birds.

Once the birds had built their nests and found sources of food and water, they began to lay their eggs, then settled in to protect them. They made only occasional day flights for food, seldom appearing before the sun had warmed the air. Those that had made fatal flaws in construction or carelessly entered or exited their nests lost an egg or two, or later a featherless chick, to the hard ground below. Lapses are not forgiven in the world of the swallows.

My elders viewed the swallows' return as an invasion, but I was always intensely interested in their survival ritual. They became my first prey, their numbers and size well matched to the firepower of my BB gun. Early photos remind me that my favorite toy was a Red Ryder, a short-barreled model I carried even before I can remember it. Like a hunter-warrior from some earlier life, I crept catlike to the end of the cookhouse, where I propped my weapon against the stucco wall and waited for a black beak and white striped head to appear. To compensate for the arc of the BB as it traveled toward the nest, I aimed an inch or so above the mud-ringed opening. I seldom hit a bird, almost never killed one. But on those few occasions when one did fall from the nest, I felt the exhilarating rush of having hit the bull's eye on a paper target.

My father's response to the annual return of these noisy little pests was more leisurely. Late in the afternoon, he sat on a chair at the end of the sheep shed with a .20-gauge single-shot Winchester propped on his lap. Like a sportsman at a trap shoot with swallows as clay pigeons, he sprayed both swallows and the windows with buckshot.

In what seemed to me to be a serious lapse of logic, he later accused me of "shooting holes in practically every damn window in the shed." When he marched me up to a window for proof by inspection, I pointed out to him that my BBs made bigger holes than those. He glanced back and forth between me and the window, and his face broke into a reluctant grin.

Donna and I always tried to save the featherless chicks that tumbled out or were nudged from their nests. If the baby bird was more than a week old and shoving itself along with its legs, opening its beak to a dropper of food, we labored to keep it alive as a pet. But not one survived. At the time, I was never much bothered by my inconsistency, that having tried to shoot the mother, I was now caring for the baby.

My response to gophers was less ambivalent. Like the adults, I saw them as interlopers. On the grassy slopes above the ranch, they dug in by the dozens, and once established in their gopher "towns," they stayed put, multiplying and expanding their territory, wiping out every blade of grass. I would sit patiently on the edge of their community and wait for a gopher in search of food or company to scurry from one hole to another. A mother would appear, vocalizing and posturing to her young to return to the tunnel. In the instant before the juvenile scurried into its hole, it would stand erect, turning its head from side to side, and I would fire one round, more often kicking up dirt from the mound beside the hole than striking the bean-shaped baby.

When I was eight years old, my father decided I had outgrown my BB gun, and he bought me a .22 Mossberg automatic rifle. A handle at the front of the barrel folded down to convert this weapon into a Tommy gun. I suppose Dad bought it because he thought that, like the automatic fishing reel, it would be easy for a boy to use. But the rifle delivered more firepower than I needed or wanted, and it was too heavy for me to hold steady even for a single firing, so I seldom made a direct hit with it. My aim was even shakier when I turned the handle down to spray my gopher prey with metal slugs, and the gun simply smoked or jammed, wasting my precious long rifle bullets.

My cousin Buddy, who lived a dozen miles down the river, once showed me what he claimed to be a surefire system for killing gophers. "All you have to do is pour a couple of pails of water into the hole. The gophers will float to the top," he told me, apparently speaking from experience. I trusted Buddy because he was several years older and he knew how to drive, but he was wrong about gophers. We hauled water most of several separate Sundays for this project, but the only gophers we saw were the few who watched from holes nearby.

Badgers I never bothered. I had seen plenty of dogs approach and even attack these carnivorous burrowers, and the confrontations were invariably either short-lived—the badger darting into its hole—or disastrous for the dog. The badger would roll over onto its back and wait for its canine victim to approach, its pit-bull jaws ready to paralyze the dog while its massive neck tensed to thrash the limp body against the ground. Badgers didn't give ground to much of anything; certainly they weren't intimidated by small boys. If I didn't leave them enough territory when I passed their burrows or happened to walk near them in the open, they would move menacingly toward me. Early on, I learned to make a wide circle around a badger.

The porcupines that built their dens in the thick underbrush near the river were more introverted. When one of these plant-eating brown balls of hair and quills was threatened or attacked, it generally rambled calmly away, arcs of miniature spears erect on its back. A dog sometimes misread these defensive movements and raced after the prey with bared teeth, only to whirl in yelping retreat the moment its mouth closed around the porcupine's armor. Ever territorial, our small dog Pal was the loser in one of these encounters, whining and pawing at her face afterward but smart enough to stand still until my father had removed a score of quills from the soft tissue around her mouth with a pair of pliers.

Although our dogs didn't go after the wild animals that lived around the ranch for food, they invariably stood their ground against any smaller creature, ready to mount an instinct-fired attack on skunk, porcupine, or badger. They almost never came away victorious from these scuffles for dominance. Fights with skunks were the worst, sending the dog home wearing its defeat in a powerful malodor that became a sweet, oniony scent. My father's big collie, Bob, his shaggy coat reeking with skunk, had to be scrubbed in the river with laundry soap more than a few times. The cats were both more practical and less ambitious, supplementing table scraps with an occasional mouse cornered in the granary, keeping alive atavistic skills that had guaranteed survival in their previous lives.

When we went after coyotes or wild dogs, it wasn't for sport. Killing these predators was work, necessary to protect our flocks. Of the many dogs that roamed the reservation, a stray on its own seldom bothered the sheep, taking chickens and rodents as its usual prey. A lobbed rock or two, maybe a rifle shot or territorial chase by a ranch dog would send these loners on their way. But when a pack of dogs, often led by a dominant bitch, hung around the edges of the ranch searching for food for their litters of pups, it was a different story. Like coyotes, a pack of wild dogs constituted a real threat to the sheep.

We spent the better part of one summer hunting down one of these packs. Led by a small, wiry black bitch with a white face and chest, the dogs had begun a reign of terror, preying at night on corralled sheep, leaving the carnage for discovery the next morning. When their marauding woke the herder, they could be driven off by a few rounds of rifle fire before they maimed or killed more than a head or two, but the next night they would be back. Unlike coyotes, which seldom take more than they can eat, this pack seemed to be killing almost for sport.

Once they were bold enough to show up on the ranch during

the day. As Jimmy Dunbar and I were walking toward the front gate after lunch, we caught sight of them through the tree shelter, prowling around near the water pump by the bunkhouse. Jimmy ran back to the house and grabbed Dad's .30-06 rifle in time to fire off a couple of futile rounds before they raced away. Had he been able to hit the lead female, the pack would probably have dispersed. The night raids continued until we moved the sheep to the mountains.

Late that summer Jimmy was returning from a visit to his father, who lived about two miles down the river, when he caught sight of these same dogs milling around the yard of an abandoned house on the first bluff below the ranch. The bitch had set up her den underneath the house and given birth to a large litter of pups there. Jimmy took me along with him when he drove back that same evening with his .22 rifle.

With our headlights and motor switched off, we rolled up close to the house in the gray twilight. Eight or ten dogs and a few pups were wandering around in the yard. Handing me a flashlight, Jimmy jumped out and shot a large male. The bitch and her pups scurried under the house while the other dogs scattered down the hill toward the river.

Jimmy took the flashlight and hurried to the hole in the foundation where the bitch had disappeared. Kneeling down, he directed the beam through the ragged opening. "We'll probably have to go get her," he said to me over his shoulder.

I was not very enthusiastic about crawling in after wild dogs, their pups, and possibly a skunk or two, so I stood outside. Jimmy wedged his way in under the house and shone the light around. "I don't see them," he stage-whispered after a moment or two. Then, forgetting to keep quiet, he called out excitedly, "Wait a minute, there's a dirt cellar in here." He backed out far enough to hand me the flashlight, instructing me to hold it straight ahead while I crawled along with him toward the dugout he had spotted in the center of the crawl space.

It was much darker under the house, but I could make out the stairs leading down from above to the cellar as we crawled along toward it. As we neared the ledge, the moving beam of my flashlight caught a pile of rags scattered across some decaying boards where the bitch crouched with two of her pups. Jimmy fired four or five times in rapid succession, killing her and one of the pups. The second pup escaped by pawing its way under a loose plank.

We backed out on our hands and knees, swinging the beam of light back and forth across the dark interior as we went. Once outside, Jimmy insisted that we look around to see if there were any more dogs still on the place. Again, I was nervous. Although there was a moon, it was fully night by now, and the only real light by which we could see into the little sheds and the barn was our single flashlight. We made a cursory search—I don't think either of us was anxious to find any more dogs—before Jimmy announced, "That's all we're going to get."

Relieved to be driving away, I felt a surge of pity for the little pup we had shot and the one we'd left to die. For that matter, I felt remorse for the bitch too. But at the same time, I couldn't deny my satisfaction that I'd helped end the rampages of the wild pack. "Now that we got her, the rest will scatter and leave," Jimmy predicted. He was right. We were never bothered by the dogs again.

Jimmy had worked as my father's foreman almost from the start, and he had become more like an uncle than just another employee, so settled in with us that he made plans to build a place of his own nearby, just above the flood plain down the river, where his father lived. He had even paid a catskinner to dig the basement for a house there. His plan was to reconcile his differences with his estranged wife and bring both her and his daughter, whom he rarely got to see, out to live in the new house while he stayed on to work at the ranch.

Reuniting his family was probably never a realistic option, but like many of the people who worked for us, he never gave up hoping to make his life whole. In spite of a checkered history that included alcoholism and drunk-tank jail time, he was unfailingly loyal, so competent at his work that my father trusted him in any situation unless it might encourage him to fall off the wagon.

Coyotes are solitary creatures. They kept to the north range and almost never ventured in near the ranch. Often when we were tending the camps, we would catch sight of one loping nearby, its fluffy tail bouncing along behind it. My father would take out his Winchester .30-06 rifle, laying the gun across the fender of the truck to steady it, and fire, but he seldom made a hit because the coyote would be half a mile away before Dad could stop, get out, and take aim.

An uglier but more exciting way to kill coyotes was to run them down with the jeep. Nimble and fast-moving, coyotes made uncertain targets until they had tired. When the chase had been successful and the wounded animal lay yelping on the ground, the coyote would take on the look of an injured pet. Dad's axe, always strapped with a shovel on the driver's side of the jeep, put it out of its pain. If the coyote appeared to be nursing a litter, we searched out the nearby den and the puppies suffered the same fate. Although the coyote's ears were worth a bounty of two dollars a pair, Dad never bothered to cut them off. This bloody ritual was easier for me to take if I had just witnessed a lamb, its flesh torn away with small tufts of wool, slowly giving ground to death.

Some killing on the ranch was part of daily work. Several times a year, and always in early summer before the shearing and haying crews came in, my father butchered yearling wethers—castrated males—for legs of lamb, shoulder roasts, and steaks and chops. In this process, he followed an invariable sequence. First he cut the yearling's throat, and then, as quickly as movement allowed, he placed hooks through the rear tendons at the knees of the back legs and hung up the carcass with a block and tackle. Moving around the carcass, he grabbed the pelt and rolled it back in his left hand as he sliced the fatty membrane between the skin and the dark red meat.

To avoid a strong muttony taste, the trick was to remove the fat along with the pelt before it could penetrate the meat. After the pelt had been removed, my father would cut the carcass with a meat saw into two halves, which were then quartered on a clean canvas before being washed and later delivered to the Cut Bank Meat Market to be wrapped and frozen. Whenever we ate lamb at a restaurant, my father would take a bite and breathe the taste into his closed mouth before passing judgment on how competently the meat had been butchered.

Our occasional encounters with pronghorn antelope, which grazed the north range in early morning and twilight, had nothing to do with work. Clocking the speed of a two-point antelope buck was pure sport for Dad and me. Passing around a butte or coming up out of a coulee when we had set out early or were returning late from tending camp, we might spot one or two young bucks that had strayed from their herd. Once sighted, they were easy to clock if Dad kept the jeep to the side a few lengths behind them, so they ran in straight lines or followed the curvature of the terrain. We often checked speedometer readings of up to forty miles per hour. Chasing an antelope could turn a bumpy ride across the range into pure adventure.

Spring

Spring was lovely on the open hill

where horses graze.

—MATTHEW HANSEN

Tending Camp

Of all the things I did with my father, what I liked best was taking supplies to the herders and moving their camps to fresh grass. Passing through our log-framed gate with the Rambouillet skull wired to its arch and heading out to the north range to tend camps, we stepped into another world. An expanse of grasslands spread out before us, more blue than green: bluestem, bluejoint, and blue gramma grasses as well as the needle grass that irritated the eyes of the sheep, coulees and high, flat-topped bluffs, Crown Butte, Antelope Hill, Horsethief Ridge, and beyond it Chalk Butte. In early summer, tiny flowers—buttercups, shooting stars, forget-me-nots—dotted the slopes we drove past.

Farther north the range became a Dakota-like badlands of white alkali flats where rainwater collected and dried in salty configurations. This was the same terrain, largely unchanged, where the Blackfeet tracked the last buffalo herds to supply the Eastern robe trade with pelts. Although the buffalo had vanished, the range was still a wildlife preserve, home to antelope and wild horses, badgers, coyotes, and gophers, field mice and jackrabbits, hawks and blackbirds and meadowlarks. It was also the winter domicile of our flocks. In the late spring, the sheep, which had been moved to Chalk Butte at the far end of the range, began their annual trek back, grazing their way across this pasturage to arrive at the ranch by shearing time.

Before my father and I left home, we would have already gone into town to pick up supplies for the herders. Our first stop was always Wilfred Nadeau's office in the back of the hardware store he owned on Main Street. Wilfred was Dad's best friend, and they always had a cup of coffee together when Dad was in town. Afterward, we ran errands—to pick up a welded piece for a mower, to buy cases of oil or chicken feed, to replace a spring leaf for the truck—before we made our final stop at the Cut Bank Meat Market, one of the few businesses on North Central Avenue that didn't sell liquor.

In the 1940s, most Montana towns, even those as small as Cut Bank, had a street or a strip where unlucky people—almost all of them men—played out their lives in a stir of booze and despair, escaping now and then to work for a few months or a season on one of the nearby ranches, in a cycle of ruin and salvation. No town actually named such a street "Skid Row," nor were the cluster of cardboard and tin shacks near the railroad bridge by the river called "Shanty Town," but that's what they were.

Bill Stephenson ran the market with his wife and their two daughters. Dad would hand his list to whichever Stephenson was behind the counter, and while the supplies (canned coffee, vegetables, and fruit; baskets of fresh apples and oranges; sacks of flour and sugar, onions and potatoes; sometimes, if I was lucky, bananas, bagged by the pound) were being loaded, he would go to his box in the freezer to pull out packages of frozen meat.

During the war, pale-blue ration stamps that came in official little books allowed the purchase of sugar, flour, coffee, and butter. The clerks at the market might spend as much time tearing out ration stamps as they did writing up the sales slip. The men who worked the ranch during the year pooled their stamps with ours, but the sheep shearers who ate there for two weeks and often left their families at home never brought along their portion of stamps. During shearing, the cooks had to make the rhubarb bitter, the gravy without butter, and the coffee weak.

As Bill tallied up the account, Dad would pull out each herder's list (Bull Durham tobacco, Zig-Zag rolling papers, Copenhagen chewing tobacco, Gillette razor blades, and Chesterfield cigarettes) and record these items and their prices under the men's names in a bound pocket tablet.

When we returned from town loaded with supplies, Mother prepared the herders' boxes. Along with his personal requests, each man got vegetables, fruit, sardines, deviled ham, Spam, and franks—all in cans—and a package or two of frozen meat or a fresh chicken packed in ice; small sacks of potatoes, onions, apples, and oranges; cookies and saltine crackers in tins; bread, oatmeal, canned milk, Log Cabin syrup, flour, wood, coal, kerosene, milk cans of water, and, most important, coffee. Some of the men actually cooked; most simply opened a can of sardines or Spam for a meal, perhaps mixing up a batch of pancakes in the morning when the stove was fired up to make coffee. Since one herder had a horse and all of the men kept a dog or two, we also put in oats and dog food.

On our way out to the sheep camps, we drove past herds of horses, the wild ones distinguishable by the stallions' flowing manes and long tails and the way they arched their necks to assert dominance over their harems of mares. Usually, several younger males and an older stallion or two would be grazing alone nearby, waiting for their time or understanding that it had past. Even the Indians didn't attempt to break these lead males when they rounded up their own herds, although they were often magnificent horses, athletic and fast.

Wild horses eat a lot of grass, in dry years competing with the sheep for what pickings there are. If it had been a dry spring, my father, Jimmy, and one of our neighbors, Brian Connelly, would have rounded up as many bands as they could find and driven them to Sundance, where they were shipped off on railroad cars to become dog and cat food or shoe leather.

A more serious threat to the grass than wild horses was fire. We kept several rolled burlap sacks under the seats of the truck and the jeep to fight grass fires started more often by hot exhaust and cigarette butts than by lightning. If the fire was small, we didn't bother dashing to the reservoir or nearest camp to get buckets of water to wet the sacks. One fire was so fast-moving we had to gather a crew and fetch rubber fire mops to put it out.

Always anxious to see what we had brought them, the herders wanted us to drive out to their bands to pick them up instead of going directly to their wagons to unload supplies. At each camp, the sheep were easier to spot than the herder. They scattered in all directions over a square mile or two. Black and undocked animals marked clusters grazing together, making it easy for the herder to keep track of the band. The herder might be on any side of the band, resting with his dog, his canvas water bag across his shoulder. Once we had found him and driven to the wagon, he would open up his supply box, pulling out each item like a birthday surprise, prolonging our visit with talk to break a solitude he otherwise seemed to enjoy.

The wagons the herders lived in looked like the ones the early settlers drove across the frontier in Western movies. The wooden frames were fifteen feet long and arched over with tightly stretched canvas, with a window at the rear and a full-sized wooden door in front. Those with wooden wheels wrapped in iron bands had been built on top of old wagons; the ones with rubber tires, on car frames. Just inside the door stood a woodstove where coffee was always brewing on the days we visited. A tin-covered opening in the roof for the vent pipe kept the canvas from catching fire.

Across from the stove, cupboards packed with canned goods stood chest high from the floor. Flypaper pulled from its cardboard cylinder hung in a yard-long spiral near the door, the lower half matted with new catches. In the middle of the wagon, a table pulled out from under the elevated bed or folded down from the side wall. Dad drank coffee with the herder there and jotted down the new order. Storage compartments with hooked latches were tucked away inside the benches and under the bed. We never stayed to watch how the herder got everything put away unless we were moving the camp to new grazing ground, and then everything had to be secured before we towed the wagon across knobs of bunch grass. The insides of the wagons and the clothes the herders wore smelled like kerosene lanterns and wood smoke. Outside, there was a woodpile with an axe sticking out of a stump next to the door. Sheep shears and bells, cresol and rope and a few blocks of salt for the sheep were kept on the side in lidded wooden boxes. An oak water barrel with a wooden spigot stood on the shade side of the wagon, and on hot days recycled water wet burlap sacks that deflected the sun.

Every band had its lead animal, usually a goat with a bell rather than one of the sheep. The lead goat would walk purposefully alongside the herder while his dog moved methodically back and forth across the rear, man and dog easily controlling a band of a thousand and more within a small perimeter. If the herder was close to camp or anxious about coyotes, he would lock the sheep away for the night inside panels wired together in a makeshift corral.

Out on the north range, coyotes were not the only thing that spooked the sheep. A formation of planes flying overhead could scatter a flock across several hundred acres as fast as a strong gust of wind whipped a field of grass, reversing all the blades at once to change its color. During the war, when a fighter plane squadron was stationed at Cut Bank, the Air Force got permission from the Blackfeet Tribal Council to use isolated parts of the reservation for target practice. The pilots set out wooden frames covered with parachute material against the sides of the tallest bluffs and used them for shelling practice from their fighter planes. After the fabric had been hit, the torn remnant beat against its frame like the wings of a bird trapped in a hayloft. Like the herders who picked up the detritus from these machine-gun firings while walking with the bands, I started my own collection of large-caliber shells linked in metal clips.

The dogs the herders kept were more than pets. All of them were highly trained sheep-guarding animals, often small black Welsh terriers with white chests and face stripes. A motion of a herder's arm accompanied by a whistle would send the dog into action. Slowly circling the band, the dog would crouch every few yards, careful not to panic the sheep, until he had coaxed together a herd that had grazed too far afield. When the herder was ready to return to his camp or to bed down the sheep in the open for the night, the dog would again slowly circle the entire herd, stopping and starting until the sheep had wrapped themselves into a tight huddle.

The most skillful ranch dog I remember—also the most love-able—was not a sheep dog but a big, hairy collie named Bob. I preferred to leave Bob at home when we went out to tend camp, but the minute he heard the truck door open, he would be up behind us. Smiling dog-style and panting in the heat of summer, when his long, matted hair must have made him miserable, he would sit upright between us, usually with his paws on the dash. If he needed more air, he leaned across me to push his head out the window, straining against the wind, his mouth dripping saliva. Every once in a while, he would get excited for no apparent reason—maybe he had caught sight of a jackrabbit—and lunge from one side to the other across our laps, licking my face, chin to forehead, in affectionate slurps when he quieted down.

Bob's great talent was his ability to follow a complex sequence of instructions. Most sheep dogs, even well-trained ones, needed the direction of a separate command for each task unless they were simply trailing sheep, a job they carried out by instinct. In contrast, Bob could carry out complicated maneuvers alone without any elaboration or coaching. My father would often send him out to bring in horses or small flocks of sheep several miles away with no more direction than a whistle or a set in the approximate direction. In an hour or so, Bob would show up with his captives in tow.

After scores of these command performances, my father didn't think twice the October afternoon he sent Bob off toward the old Monroe place to bring back a small mixed hospital band of young wethers and ewes held back for various health reasons after most of the sheep had been sent to fall market. When night fell and the dog had not reappeared with the flock, my father went out to look for him. He found only the sheep.

For days afterward, Dad searched for Bob. Even weeks later, my father still contended that Bob had been injured and that he was holing up somewhere until he was in good enough shape to hobble home. But Bob never reappeared, and we never found his body. In the end, my father decided that he had been shot, then crawled into some sheltered place to die. He never replaced Bob.

The men who chose to isolate themselves on the range with a band of sheep and a dog were not necessarily an asocial lot; on the contrary, they bear witness to how little company a man really needs to get along. Some were immigrants from sheep-raising countries like Norway or Spain, men who had turned back to the only skills they had to make their livelihoods and put their wages aside to make their own stakes. Some were alcoholics whose only refuge from this curse came from self-imposed exile on a ranch or a road crew, the railroad or a logging gang. Others had simply gone into hiding from lives that had turned sour with divorce or dysfunction or poverty, or they were escaping from criminal histories that kept them from competing for regular jobs in town.

The only time I can remember seeing my father afraid—openly apprehensive about an event he felt he might not be able to handle—involved a herder from this last category. After Dad had hired the man to herd a band near Horsethief Ridge, he picked up a rumor in town from one of the men who hung out in the Glacier Bar that the herder had served time in the state penitentiary for cutting up another camp tender with an axe. My father always carried a rifle on his trips north but never a weapon to be used on a man. I didn't know he even owned a pistol; perhaps he had borrowed the .32 short-barreled model he threw into the glove compartment the day we drove out to Horsethief Ridge to fire the herder.

My father didn't say anything to me about the herder on the ride out to the range. As we approached the camp, he stubbed out his cigarette in the ashtray and rolled down his window deliberately. Shifting into a lower gear, he opened the glove compartment and lifted the pistol out of its leather holster. "Get in the back as soon as I stop the truck," he told me quietly. "Don't worry about trying to close the door." Whenever he said not to worry about something, I understood that he meant not to do it.

While I scrambled into the back, he got out of the truck, leaving the pistol on the front seat, and walked slowly toward the herder, keeping himself between the open truck door and the wagon. I crouched down and looked through the back window of the cab to see what was going on. The first thing I caught sight of, framed in the front windshield, was a chopping stump with a long-handled axe sticking out of it. I was worried.

My father seemed to be doing most of the talking, but I couldn't make out much of what the two men were saying. After a few moments, the herder started nodding, rocking back and forth almost, in what seemed to be resigned agreement. Still facing the herder, my father moved backward past the open door and lifted out the box of supplies we had brought along. Then, he walked back toward the wagon, set the supplies down next to the chopping block, turned and strode back to the truck, signaling me with a wave of his hand to get into the cab. I crawled over the side of the bed and into the cab just in time to pull the door shut before he began to back the truck down the short incline.

Only after we had turned around did Dad put the pistol in its holster and shove it back into the glove compartment. After a mile or so, he said, half to himself, "I probably shouldn't have brought you along." And then, still thinking out loud, "Jimmy can pick him up and take him to town when he brings the new man out." Both of us were relieved.

Some herders, men like Andy Reishoff, were simply eccentrics, loners who seemed to adapt best to life when they were on their own. Andy himself was a bright if unorthodox fellow who never said much but always wore an agreeable expression. Grains of the Skoal tobacco he chewed stuck to the hairs of his unshaven face and mustache where the wind had interrupted the intended trajectory of his spit. His teeth were dark with tobacco stains, the brown tracings extended into the lines around his mouth. Andy always seemed to be wearing all of his clothes at once, regardless of the barometric readings—army surplus sweaters pulled over wool shirts, topped by a heavy, square-patched, wool coat, a full set of long johns under everything. His favorite headgear was a wool-lined bomber's hat with ear flaps, tied now at the chin, now over the top.

Andy was also the only herder with a horse, a red sorrel that my father had given up on as unbreakable. Although the sorrel was easily the fastest horse on the ranch and certainly the hardest to handle, when Andy rode him, he was as docile as one of the sheep, moving along the same way Andy did, slowly and deliberately. Andy was as comfortable with machines as he was with animals. In fact, he was a man in love with technology. He was the only herder we knew who hooked up an electric generator driven by a gasoline engine to operate the lights and heater he wired into his wagon. Unlike most of the men, who might on occasion page through an outdated copy of *Reader's Digest*, Andy actually subscribed to *The National Geographic* and *The Saturday Evening Post*, which he piled up in orderly stacks next to his bed along with the mail-order catalogs from Sears and Roebuck and Montgomery Ward. He pored over articles detailing future technological wonders—a self-assembled one-man aircraft, for example—and ordered himself gadgets like a seven-in-one pocket knife.

His most novel purchase, and one I lusted after, was a scooter with the trade name Doodle Bug. A miniature rubber-tired dynamo with one forward gear and a gasoline engine that started with a kick-down pedal, it was the ideal vehicle for an innovative herder to use to skirt the perimeters of his band. On my most disappointing Christmas I had ordered the Doodle Bug through petitions to Santa Claus, my parents, and even God. I received instead a red Zenith bicycle with fat tires, a gift that permanently undermined my faith in both Santa Claus and prayer.

Although my father never bought a Doodle Bug, he did acquire a half-dozen other vehicles for the ranch, including a Ford coupe, a pickup, a two-ton cab-over truck, and a jeep and a Dodge weapons carrier from military surplus. If we were taking a load of panels or water to all the camps, my father would drive the big truck. When I was younger, I often lay with my head in his lap on the long rides to

At the wheel of the jeep, 1947

and from the north range, alternately dozing and jerking alert when we rolled over a bump in the road or stopped to open a gate. He would cradle my head with his right hand so I didn't lean into the oversized steering wheel when he braked or drove down a steep or rough incline. I seldom got through the long ride home without a nap.

It was harder to sleep in the jeep. Its bucket seats forced me to sit up straight, and during the summer months when we removed the doors, pitching out onto the prairie was a danger if I nodded off. But as I got older and didn't nap as much, I preferred to take the jeep when we went to tend camp because it increased my chances of being allowed to drive back.

I started driving around the ranch the winter I was seven. My father set the throttle on the big truck at a fast idle so I could steer it kneeling on the seat while he unloaded hay or oil cake for the sheep off the back. Thus I took over one of my mother's old jobs. The next summer, he taught me how to drive the jeep, more suited to my size and easier to handle. Still, in the beginning, I had to hang on to the wheel while I slid down a few inches in the seat to depress the clutch far enough to shift the gears. Since the shifting stroke was a short one, I needed to move it only the width of my hand. The brake pedal was easier to reach and had to be depressed just a few inches. The emergency hand brake came out of the dash where I could easily reach it with my right hand. All the gauges and instruments there glowed a florescent green in the dark.

For several years after I had learned to drive, I couldn't understand why my father waited for me to ask to take the wheel rather than stopping and saying, "It's your turn now." I would worry and wait for the perfect moment—stopping to open a gate, for instance—before asking, "Dad, want me to drive through?" If we were not on a hill, he generally smiled and let me take over. But I could never bring myself to say, "Damn it, Dad, stop and let me drive." He concentrated so intently when he was working that I guess I felt it wasn't acceptable to interrupt unless there was a natural break. Once I took the wheel, I stayed in the driver's seat the rest of the way home.

Though there was no play I liked better than driving along on the back roads and on the open range, my role models for driving were not my father or even Jimmy, who always leaned harder on the gas pedal than Dad, but rather the teenage drivers I had studied in Cut Bank. During the winter, the high school boys in town would try to maneuver their cars around on the icy streets without using their brakes. When they approached a stop sign, they braked just long enough to slip the gear shift gently into reverse. While the rate of slowdown was dictated by the speed of the wheels, their backward motion stopped the car. The best stops were slow and easy—cool stops, I judged. Watching one of these performances, I would marvel at the physics of the car's forward thrust in counteraction with the spinning restraints of the wheels.

My attempts to imitate this maneuver were largely unsuccessful, and the alarming grind of the gears made me a little apprehensive about trick driving. The driver's stance that I did manage to affect was sliding to the left with a slight twist to lodge my left shoulder and chest between the door and the steering wheel while nonchalantly resting my right hand on top of the wheel. From that position, I could look over my shoulder at the outside world or perhaps, I thought, even drive without taking my eye off an imagined girl passenger, except for a quick glance now and then toward the road. My father would query me with his puzzled and a little annoyed look: "What are you doing?" Instead of answering, I would sit up quickly, pretending I had been leaning over to pick something up off the floor.

Lambing

My father used to say he never understood how sheep managed to survive before we were around to take care of them. During lambing, which went on for a full hectic month in the spring, we all understood what he meant. Birthing ewes often refused to cooperate in the process, continuing to run with the flock even after the lamb's head had begun to emerge. My mother was often called out to assist in a stalled labor or a breach delivery, since her hands and arms were small enough to reach forcepslike into the birth canal and move the lamb's head along far enough to get a strap around its jaw or feet. If a stillborn lamb had been dead for awhile, the smell was so foul it made us choke.

Each healthy drop was hand-carried to one of the eight compartments in the low-riding lambing wagon standing by. Some mother ewes could be coaxed along, sniffing their lambs; others running loose with the rest of the flock had to be hooked with a shepherd's staff or sheep hook and shoved up a plank to join their newborns. When these maternity pairs were later driven to small pens in the sheep shed, the job was often just beginning. Bonding in sheep is an uncertain business, the instinctive connection directed almost entirely by smell, and even after the ewe was isolated with her lamb, she might well kick away the unsteady drop when it tried to nurse.

Jimmy Dunbar always handled the difficult cases. On watch in the sheep shed, he patrolled the aisles between stalls, stopping whenever there was trouble to hold a ewe against the side of the pen while he shoved her teat into the lamb's mouth. Twins and triplets always required his attention.

When a lamb died or was stillborn, Jimmy used pure slight of hand to persuade the lactating ewe to accept another ewe's twin as her own. He would skin the dead lamb, then fit its warm pelt onto a wobbly twin before setting it down in a pen with the lambless ewe. After a moment or two of nervous cruising, the ewe would stand still just long enough for the lamb to begin to suckle before she pulled away. When this dance of guarded acceptance had been repeated three or four times—Jimmy always stood by to make sure that the jacket stayed put—the ewe would finally settle down while the lamb eagerly hammered its head into her breast to stimulate the flow of milk. Only the next morning when Jimmy was satisfied that he had successfully brokered the adoption did he paint the pair with corresponding numbers, which might outlast their kinship after all.

Once the troubled bondings had been sorted out and the lambs were a week old, they had to be moved again to free up stalls in the sheep shed for more recent drops. The established pairs of ewes and lambs were first put in holding pens behind the sheep shed, then a few days later they were taken in a small band to pasture with a herder on the slopes near the ranch. Only after we had sheared all the ewes and castrated and docked their lambs did we trail the flocks to their summer pasturage.

Always methodical in his work habits, my father set up a virtual assembly line for castrating the male lambs and docking the tails of all of the new additions to the flock. Presiding with a sharp knife at a board nailed diagonally across a corner panel in the corral, he waited for Jimmy to present the squirming underside of each lamb. Jimmy would drag a male from the adjoining corral, pulling its front and hind legs together on each side, and lift it onto the board. After my father had sliced off the tip of the lamb's scrotum and worked the testes out of the sack until they were partially exposed, he bent to pull them out one at a time with his teeth. To shorten a lamb's tail to two inches, he used the same knife, sealing the spurting veins with a hot iron. Stationed beside him on a box, I dipped cresol from a can and painted each scrotum sac and tail stub to prevent infection. Finally, another hand released the lamb into a second corral.

Years later, I could still remember this ritual in such detail that, with no experience beyond my observations in middle childhood, I was able to give a full demonstration of castrating and docking lambs for my high school animal husbandry class. At the time, I liked a girl whose brother owned the lambs and she had seemed to return my interest, but after witnessing my compelling performance, she avoided me and turned her attention to another boy.

In the war years, when most able-bodied ranch hands had enlisted or been drafted, one of the biggest headaches during the frenetic month of lambing was hiring and holding onto a crew. Even though my father could usually go into Cut Bank and round up a crew at the Smoke House or Connelly's Bar—men who held themselves out as willing to work for the month—these temporary hands were always alcoholics, often poor drifters with no work records, perhaps not so much as a birth certificate, and so unreliable that some would quit or wander off after a week or two or, if they stayed on, cause trouble of one kind or another.

In the spring of 1943, a week after lambing had begun, one of the men hired to patrol the sheep shed at night and keep an eye out for trouble among the new drops disappeared with no warning. Desperate to replace him, my father had to go into town twice before he found a new hand, a strangely aloof fellow who wore carpenter's pants with a blackjack stuck in the ruler slot and a permanent scowl. He rarely spoke except to complain about the work hours or the food.

Besides being generally disagreeable, the new night herder

couldn't be trusted to follow basic safety rules. Twice during the first week of his stay he had left a lighted lantern sitting on a bed of straw in the sheep shed when he went out for his break. Jimmy said he was "just plain no good" and should be let go, but, short-handed as we were, he finally agreed with my father that a firm reprimand might be a better course. The stage was set for the trouble that followed when several evenings later the herder made a scene at supper over the coffee.

At almost every meal during his stay with us, the herder had complained, usually just muttering to himself, that the coffee was weak. It was true that rationing was tight and the cook had adjusted to our reduced supply. This night in the cookhouse, the herder suddenly slammed down his cup and announced angrily that he couldn't drink anymore of this "one-ground-a-cup bilge" before pushing away from the table and slamming out of the room. My father didn't say a word but as soon as he had finished eating, he got up and followed the herder out to the sheep shed.

My sister and I often played in the sheep shed after dinner in the long twilights. Since we couldn't open the heavy panels blocking the doorway, we gained our access by crawling up over the top. That evening, even before we had pulled ourselves up onto the panel of the shearing wing, we could hear the angry exchange between my father and the herder. We arrived just in time to see the last round of this confrontation.

No sooner had we perched ourselves on the panel than the herder reached for a pair of sheep shears stuck in the wall. Closing them to form a spear of overlapping scissors, he drew back his right arm and thrust it at my father's chest. Turning quickly and raising his right hand to shield himself, Dad caught the blades of the shears with his splayed hand. Blood gushed from the deep gash opened in the fleshy pad near his thumb. The conflict exploded.

My father rushed the herder and grabbed him around the arms and shoulders. When the herder broke loose, Dad chased him into the rows of lambing pens in the main section of the sheep shed. By the time we caught up with them, my father had shoved the man down midaisle between the pens; balancing himself against the rail with his uninjured hand, he was stomping the daylights out of him. The herder crumbled into a ball on the floor, grunting as he tried to protect his face and stomach from my father's kicks. Dad wore high-topped White logging boots with the cowboy's slanted heel, a shoe design as effective for this kind of work as for holding a foot in the stirrup. He stopped kicking when Jimmy came running from the other side of the shed.

The two of them pulled the herder to his feet and marched him outside toward the bunkhouse. His head and shoulders were soaked with blood, most of it from my father's hand. Donna and I raced back to the house and waited for my father, following him into the kitchen when he reappeared. Mother let out a short scream when she saw all the blood and covered her mouth with her hand. After Dad had calmed her down and cleaned the gash with iodine and bandaged it up, he set out again for the bunkhouse, this time in the pickup.

Jimmy was waiting for him outside on the steps. When my father pulled up, he stuck his head inside and the herder appeared, carrying his bedroll and a suitcase. Dad put his left hand firmly on the back of the herder's neck as he staggered down the steps and shoved him toward the pickup. Instead of dropping the man off at the Glacier Bar, Dad drove him to the jail in Cut Bank. He would be held overnight and given what everybody in those days called "walking papers" when the sheriff dropped him off the next morning at the "Welcome to Cut Bank" sign on the edge of town. As far as we knew, the man never showed up in town again, and my father and Jimmy managed to get through the rest of the month without hiring anyone else.

As it turned out, 1943 was the last year we had to worry about getting a reliable crew together for lambing. By the middle years of the war, the demand for wool had grown greater than the demand for meat. About the same time, many sheep ranchers in the western states had begun to expand their herds. Adjusting to these changes in the market, my father simply got out of the lambing business and started to contract for lambs to be delivered in the fall when they were four or five months old; then he would shear them early the next summer. After he had bred the ewes, he sent them off to Utah to swell the herds run by the Mormon ranchers there. The wethers he shipped to Kentucky, where they were fattened on the leftovers of the tobacco harvest. By early December they would arrive in New York in time to be butchered for the holidays.

Shearing

Excitement always grew around Memorial Day, as we waited for the caravan of pre-war Dodge cars and Ford pickups and aerodynamic plywood trailers that signaled the arrival of the shearers. A smaller crew would have already come in to do the tagging—removing the wool around the sheep's eyes so they could see to graze and around their buttocks to prevent fly eggs from hatching there—but shearing was the big event. Unlike the men hired to work during lambing, the shearing crew were all professionals. Some came all the way from Mexico, but most of them were locals whose families hailed from sheep-raising countries like New Zealand and Wales and Ireland.

Even in years when the river hadn't flooded, it was a struggle for the shearers to maneuver their vehicles along the low-lying dirt road and get across the narrow cable bridge. Once safely on the ranch side, the party made camp along the red lath-and-wire snow fence that quarter-circled the area behind the cookhouse. Here, the shearers who had brought their families with them would put up their big white tents with cookstoves near the front flaps and metal stove pipes poking through the roofs. The single shearers and those traveling in pairs slept rough, usually in the back of their pickups.

My father would have gone down to Great Falls several weeks before the shearing crews arrived to find a cook from among the ranks of hotel and ex-military chefs who hired on at ranches now and again for a few weeks' change of scene. Mother and a woman brought in to help her would clean the cookhouse, stock the pantry with food, and get Jimmy to bring in wood for the stove. While the cookhouse and the shearing wing of the sheep shed were being prepared, the herders would begin to move the sheep in toward the ranch where they could be divided into smaller groups spaced to match the rate of shearing.

During the war, when we were short-handed, I would be entrusted to bring a small band in the last few miles. On these occasions Dad dropped me off on a grazing slope several miles from the ranch. There, I would dash back and forth around the straggling rear flanks of a little band, shaking a ring of tin cans strung on a wire to keep the sheep moving along toward home, instructed as usual not to loiter along the way. One day when I had been recruited for this job, the stiff backs of the new oxfords I was wearing rubbed blisters on my heels before I had traveled half a mile. Stumbling along behind the sheep with my rattle of cans, I saw the rolling dust cloud of a truck speeding toward me.

"What in the hell have you been doing out here?" my father demanded after he had pulled up in an irregular stop.

"Trying to walk," I replied tearfully.

He loaded me into the truck and we raced back to pick up someone else to finish the job. Later, when the herd had been tucked away in the corral behind the sheep shed, my father noticed that I was still limping around in the yard, duty-bound to break in the new oxfords.

"Give me those damn shoes," he ordered impatiently, and walking to the edge of the coral, he threw the offending pair into the river. "Tell your mother to buy you shoes that fit," he said on his return. Although the oxfords we bought at Larson's Department Store in Cut Bank were always scientifically sized by an X-ray machine that revealed the ghostly bones of my feet, a pair of comfortable shoes was a luxury I rarely enjoyed during those years.

As soon as the shearers had settled into their camp, they set up their equipment. Motors with jointed gear arms to drive the wide, long-toothed clippers were hooked up next to the six-foot-square platforms that extended from the ten stalls out into the shearing wing of the shed. Two wool sacks hung up like a pair of drawn curtains separated each platform from the rear of the stall, where three or four adult sheep would be deposited at a time to wait their turns with the clippers. Deflated tire tubes were suspended from the rafters by ropes with counterweights so the shearers could lean forward into them to support their backs. At the end of each shearing day, my sister and I, finding play everywhere, would swing in these inner tubes, doubling up our small frames to set the heaviest ones in motion.

Shearing itself was a spectacle no one wanted to miss. While the sheep shed echoed with the plaintive bleatings, unremitting and overlapping, of hundreds of animals issuing distress calls to one another, the women from the house and friends from town and neighboring ranches often stood in the space behind the first panel inside the door to watch. Paid by the number of sheep they handled, the shearers worked with dexterity and precision, moving across the stages of their stalls as nimbly as acrobats.

After the shearer had reached through the burlap curtains to drag a sheep onto the stage, he trimmed first the legs, next the forehead, and then, with downward strokes, the chest and edges of the stomach. Once the chest was clean, the shearer cradled the sheep against his leg with one arm while his other hand directed the clippers upward from chest to neck, trimming the chin and the area behind the ears. Finally, he would lay the sheep down, first on one side, then the other, to peel the wool—yellowish near the skin—in long strokes from the buttocks, the back, and the neck. Once captured, the sheep always submitted passively to the shearing ritual.

Released at last, the denuded sheep would regain its unsteady feet and slip across the lanolin-slick floor to freedom. The shearer would hang up his clippers and slowly straighten out his back, stretching his neck and shoulders as he pushed the pile of fresh wool toward the front edge of the boardwalk with his feet. After adding a chalk mark to his tally, in a single continuous motion he would part the curtains to pull the next sheep by the leg onto the wood planks as he leaned forward again into his swing.

The sharp, high-speed clippers often nicked the sheep's loose skin, which hangs in folds and ripples into deep creases when the animals are turned and positioned during shearing. My father would grow impatient if a shearer didn't show enough regard for the sheep, cutting deep gashes along with the unavoidable nicks. He cleaned and disinfected these wounds and sewed them up with a curved needle and surgical thread. If any shearer had cut several sheep in succession, he approached the head man and warned him that such negligence had to stop.

While the shearers worked, my father or Jimmy stationed himself across from the stalls near the sliding door through which the shearlings leaped into the holding corral. Here, one or the other notched a panel in scores of ten to record the number sheared, and at the end of the day, my father would reconcile his own count with the head shearer's. They treated nicks and sewed up gashes, and finally branded each animal's back, off center and to the right, with a triangle in permanent yellow paint. The tool that impressed this brand was a crude affair, a bent tomato can nailed to a tapered handle.

The men who scooped up the fresh wool from the stages and tied it into bundles wore leather gloves with the fingers cut out to the second joint. Tying wool is as hard on the hands as it is on the back. They wrapped thick skeins of pre-cut twine around their waists, folded over in back like the belts of Sumo wrestlers. Pulling a single three-foot strand from his belt, the tier would bend to lay it across his boots, fold the fleece from a single sheep into a tight ball on top of the twine, and tie and cross-tie the bundle.

Now and again throughout the day, my father traveled the length of the shearing wing, stopping in front of each stall to weigh the bundles piled up there, happy when his hand-held Chatillon scale registered at least eight pounds. After the tier had secured half a dozen fleeces, he lugged them to the end of the row of stalls and threw them one at a time up onto the ten-foot-high stomper's platform. Like every boy on a sheep ranch, I felt I had come of age when, at eight, I first managed to hoist a bundle of wool up onto the stage in a single try.

On the stomper's platform, huge burlap sacks were secured by a metal ring and lowered through a three-foot hole cut in the center of the floor. Before a sack was pushed through the hole, the bottom corners were filled with wool and tied with twine into ears. These handles allowed the men to move the sacks once they had been packed with wool. The stomper stood inside the giant sack that hung from the platform and tamped down the fleeces tossed in to him. Starting at the outer edges, he worked his way toward the center of the sack and back out again until he had packed his way to the top. An autocrat in this burlap domain, he controlled the pace of delivery by calling out for each pair of bundles, protesting loudly if one of the tiers tried to break the monotony with a little horse-play and tossed fleeces like basketballs into the sack. Once the sack was a third full and the stomper could reach bundles on the platform, he pulled them in himself, two at a time.

When a sack was full, it was hoisted onto a heavy board so that the ring could be removed and the opening sewn shut. Finally, it would be dropped over the side of the platform to be weighed. Before the sacks were piled up, four to a stack, my father himself marked and circled the weight of each one in indelible paint. At sale time, the buyer's numbers had to match his or he would demand a second weighing.

At the start of each sack, I was often assigned the job of rolling the bundles of wool two at a time down into the sack on call. Sitting on the ring with one leg dangling into the hole, I breathed in the mixed pungency of wool and burlap and passed the moments between calls checking for ticks.

Although ticks show up wherever there are sheep, during shearing they were especially bothersome, attaching themselves to anything warm and moist. I would find them clinging to my socks, sometimes see them crawling up my leg when I lifted my trouser cuff. If I discovered a tick embedded in my skin, my mother would sterilize a sewing needle with a lighted match, then apply it to the exposed abdomen of the tick. When the tick felt the hot needle, it would back slowly out, sometimes needing the encouragement of several applications to complete its measured retreat.

We knew that ticks could carry disease—everybody had heard of deadly Rocky Mountain spotted fever—but no one in those days worried much about it. And although my father was solicitous about the comfort of pregnant women and old people and, of course, worried about the well-being of his animals, he paid almost no attention to matters of personal health. We were simply not supposed to get sick. Like most rural people then, he equated sickness with weakness.

If the stomper's sack was less than a quarter full at the end of the day, I would climb down into it when the crew stopped work and sway back and forth for the fun of it. Getting out again was never easy, even when I had had the foresight to tie a shinny rope to the platform fence and take it along with me into my burlap swing.

Another of our favorite playgrounds was the corner of the shed where the filled wool sacks piled up. Here, my sister and I chased each other across sacks the size of bloated whales, using the ears sticking out from the corners as handholds to clamber up and down. Here, we played thrilling, almost frenzied rounds of hide-and-seek in the narrow alleyways between stacks. As I slithered down between two piles to hide, my shirt would bunch up to expose my back to the rough burlap. The reek of wool and burlap was so overpowering I panted to keep from choking, literally breathless, as I waited for Donna to discover me.

When one of us got caught in a hiding place deep in the mountain of sacks, our play would reach a nearly hysterical pitch as the other descended again and again in failed rescue attempts. Neither of us wanted to call for help—our makeshift jungle gym would surely be put off limits—so on those occasions when Jimmy or one of the pen wranglers finally had to be summoned to pull us out, we always insisted on his promise not to tell. In the years after the war, when wool prices were down and the sacks stayed stored in the shed for months after shearing, we played there well into the autumn.

At the end of their long work days, the shearers built smoke fires around their camp to discourage the mosquitoes that bred in the stagnant water along the river banks. Then, after dinner in the long Montana twilights, they played baseball, inning after inning, on equal opportunity teams, each required to incorporate a child or two. When it was finally too dark to play, or if the mosquitoes had won out, we lingered awhile longer around the fires, visiting and telling stories, savoring the long summer evening.

After the last sheep had been sheared and the camp was broken up, the shearers' caravan of cars and trucks and campers made its way back across the bridge and up the dirt road to the highway. When the shearers had gone, Donna and I would search the grass around their abandoned campsite for coins and jackknives and other treasures left behind. For a day or two, the ranch would seem unnaturally quiet.

Summer

Opened, clear as child's geography,

The summer countries, the hills

Folding and unfolding.

—HENRY RAGO

Trailing to Heart Butte

Sheep are, first of all, sheep, as anyone who tends them will tell you, followers in fact as well as in proverb. With this axiom in mind, my father began the yearly trip with our bands to their summer home in the mountain foothills by inaugurating a leader of the flock, almost always a goat rather than one of the sheep. When he tied a bell around the neck of this animal, he also greased the deal with a few pellets of oil cake in a tin lard bucket. Once Nanny had been persuaded to fall in at his side, the sheep could be counted on to trail along behind her.

Our destination was the Great Bear Wilderness Range, which lay west of Heart Butte between Browning and Dupuyer. To get there, we trailed the sheep for four days over a thirty-mile obstacle course with my father at the lead in the jeep, Jimmy and a few other men riding horseback up and down the flanks to keep the line tight, and a single herder—usually Andy, sometimes on his red sorrel, always with his dog—crisscrossing at the rear. Thus on parade, we would set out for the summer pasturage a week or so after the shearers had finished their work.

The first trial arose when we were barely underway, at the edge of the river. Even when the water was unseasonably low and the sheep could be cajoled to wade, to swim even, across the gravel-bottomed shallows, we had to keep an eye on the weaker animals. Older ewes held over might slip on the rocks; undersized yearlings could get caught in the current. But this early in the summer the river almost always ran high, forcing us to spend the better part of the first day coaxing the sheep through a funnel of panels onto the wobbly cable bridge. Invariably, the animals crowded toward the center of this narrow span (our sheep hadn't any instinct for the protocol Noah taught their forebears), with those on the flanks frantically butting the ones caught in the middle. Before the flock could be herded across and realigned on the opposite bank, a dozen or so of the frailest would be pushed over the side and more often than not lost in the water below.

If we had used up the day in a laborious crossing, my father would leave the flock to graze on the pasture above the ranch, bedding them down later in the evening near the bluffs along the river. If we had made it across the river by early afternoon, he would press on to Blackfoot, where the sheep bedded near the stockyards. In either case, several herders stayed to spend the night with the flock while the rest of us returned to the ranch for supper.

Early the next morning we would set out again from home and, after delivering the night herders their breakfast, trail the sheep for five miles along the edge of Highway 2. This easy stretch ended abruptly at the Y below Browning, where we had to get the flock across the highway. To carry out this feat, my father stationed a man a quarter of a mile away in each direction to flag down cars while the sheep streamed across the road. When I was assigned one of these posts, he tied his handkerchief to a stick that I waved so that approaching drivers would be sure to see me.

Even in those more relaxed times, we encountered plenty of travelers who impatiently beeped their horns at us or, hell-bent to continue on their way, nosed their cars in and out through the milling sheep like taxi drivers on a Calcutta street. In such cases, my father simply capitulated, splitting the band and waving the cars on by.

By late afternoon, we would reach Two Medicine Creek, where all of us spent the night in the open with the flock. Since that area was more for cattle and horses, rather than sheep country, Dad and I would drive ahead to ask permission from a local rancher to set up camp on his land. On those occasions when we were turned away, we were obliged to trail the sheep farther along the ditch until we found a more gracious host.

By the time the flock had been watered, grazed, and bedded down for the night, our supper would have arrived, towed out from the ranch in a sheep wagon. No food was ever more appetizing to me than the fried chicken and potato salad and tinned beans dished out at these open-air meals, which I ate from a paper plate with ridged partitions that ingeniously segregated one ration from another. No entertainment was more exciting than the stories, tales of ill-fated encounters with wild animals and crazed herders the men vied to tell in the time between supper and sleep. Sprawled on the tailgate, I hung on their words, and hours after the last voice had stilled, gruesome and terrifying figures from these lurid recitals crowded my dreams.

I will admit now, as perhaps I knew even then, that most of the yarns spun out into these summer evenings were apocryphal, fragments of a mountain-camp folklore largely compounded of rampaging bears and human madness. Nevertheless, I will attest to the truth of a representative pair, both of them tales my father himself vouched for when he sometimes entered into the after-dinner storytelling contests. They dated from his days on the Johnny Sullivan ranch near Pendroy, and one of them featured him in a central role.

During my father's time with the Sullivans, a camp tender returning from his rounds brought back word that one of the herders had gone berserk. Johnny took my father along when he rode up to verify this report, planning to bring the man in if it were true. In fact, the herder had gone mad in his mountain isolation. When Johnny and my father approached his camp, he emerged from his wagon, raving incoherently and brandishing a shotgun at them. The two men called out to him from a distance for a while, with no success. Finally, my father announced that if he could talk to the herder at closer range, he could persuade him to put down his weapon and come along quietly.

My father started slowly toward the crazed man, talking as he walked, but before he had come within twenty feet of the wagon, the herder opened fire. The force of the blast knocked my father to the ground, and later in Browning a doctor labored for hours to pick the number-6 buckshot (designed for smaller game) out of his skin. Years afterward, an embedded BB still surfaced now and then on his chest. In the end, it was the sheriff from Choteau who got the job of bringing the crazy herder into the state hospital at Warm Springs.

The second story my father told also involved one of the Sullivan herders, a man who was mauled almost to death when he went out to check a night noise he thought was his horse tangled in its halter rope. He encountered a bear instead. Contrary to popular lore, bear attacks were not common in the wilderness areas during the summer unless a herder had been careless about storing his food or disposing of his garbage. Common sense had it that you never cooked bacon in the camp. When a bear did wander into a camp at night, a shotgun blast over its head would usually serve to move it along to new feeding grounds. So, when the Sullivan herder saw the source of the disturbance on this night and fired into the air, he was acting in line with accepted wisdom.

Instead of fleeing, this bear charged, retreated, and charged several more times after knocking the man to the ground with one swipe of its huge paw. Then it hung around, first to rip the flesh on his back with its claws and then nearly to paralyze his right arm and shoulder with its incisors. After the bear had finally lumbered off, the man lay motionless in the pool of his gore, terrified

Band of sheep on the north range

the animal might return to cover its prey. Finally, near dawn, he dragged himself back to his wagon, where he tried to wrap up his wounds and prayed that someone—a camp tender, a ranger— would find him before he bled to death. By good chance, another herder rode by the wagon that morning in time to rescue him.

The third trailing day was easy going, especially after we got past the junction seven miles above Heart Butte early in the afternoon. Now we were moving into the foothills along little-traveled roads, passing streams where the sheep could drink as they went along.

That evening we bedded the flock down just outside the town of Heart Butte. Many members of the Blackfeet Tribe lived in this district, both in the tiny town and on its fringes, where the government had set up model agricultural teaching programs for them in the 1920s. Heart Butte itself, the most traditional Indian community in northwestern Montana, amounted to a general store with its post office, a corral for pack horses, half a dozen tepees, a few houses, and the Blackfeet round hall, a moonlight school where craft and vocational classes were still offered.

On the last leg of the trail, we traveled well up into the foothills, where the dirt roads tapered into rutted, one-lane logging paths, until we reached the Great Bear Wilderness. On the fourth morning, before we headed west out of Heart Butte into this new terrain, where coyotes were more likely to appear and keeping the sheep together was trickier than on the plains, my father divided up the flock into smaller bands, each with its own herder.

As we climbed the grassy hillsides and crossed pine-fringed meadows, I would breathe in the sharp, piney scent of tamarack and ponderosa, reach down to pluck a dogtooth violet or a sprig of Indian paintbrush, or to rub my hand up and down against the tight cone of tiny flowers that shape the spear bloom of bear grass. The sheep dogs would flush bevies of sage grouse, cackling like guinea fowl, out of the serviceberry bushes. Squirrels and chipmunks, fearless of human trespassers, darted about, hurrying through the brief mountain summer to store winter food.

On these days, it never struck me as at all strange that a man might want to spend a few months alone each year in this place near the top of the world. Just before we left for home, my father would remind the herders to keep an eye out for lupine poisoning in the sheep during the first weeks of August, when the plants formed their bean-filled pods.

Indian Days

Two different stories have been offered to account for how the Blackfeet got their tribal name. The more prosaic explanation is that the moccasins of the three tribes of Great Lakes Indians who migrated across the prairies and plains in the seventeenth century, first to Alberta and later in smaller bands from there to Montana, became soiled, or literally "blackened," by the scorched earth they traversed in their journeys. The older and more fabulous account recalls a legendary chief who sent the oldest of his three sons to hunt buffalo he had seen in a dream. Following the instructions laid out in his father's vision, the novice hunter found the buffalo— thousands of them—right away but was still at a loss as to how to go at them until the Sun appeared in a second vision to supply him with a black medicine to paint his feet. His descendants took their name from this magic, which empowered him to stampede the buffalo and become a great hunter, and each year when the prairie grass was greenest, they renewed their allegiance to the Sun in a sacred dance of thanksgiving. This same Sun Dance was reenacted as the central event at the powwow hosted in Browning early each July by the tribes of the Blackfeet Nation—the Siksikas and the Kainahs from Alberta and the Montana Piegans.

The Piegans were once known as the fiercest warriors of all the Plains Indians, hostilely aggressive to nearby tribes including the Assiniboine and the Crow. After they migrated south from Alberta in the eighteenth century, they controlled all the land north of the Yellowstone River between the Continental Divide and the North Dakota border for over a hundred years. By the beginning of this century, this huge territory encompassing most of northern Montana had long since been surrendered to mining, railroad, timber, and ranching interests, whittled down by conquest and treaty to fewer than a million and a half acres of reservation, a third of even that remnant owned by white interlopers. Their numbers diminished by starvation and small pox, most of the Montana Blackfeet who had survived these encroachments now lived in the western part of the reservation, in and around Browning, where, warriors no more, they welcomed neighboring tribes—Nez Percé, Kutenai, Pend d'Oreille, Atsina, and Assiniboine—to join them in a weeklong midsummer conclave.

In a final irony of cultural assimilation, early in this century the tribal gathering had been incorporated into the white celebration of Independence Day, the heathen singing and dancing, mock battles, and prayers softened and made more acceptable to missionaries and Indian Service bureaucrats by an accompaniment of American flags and ice cream and parades. The later addition of a rodeo ensured local commercial interests that the event would become one of the area's main tourist attractions. Like everyone else who lived within a hundred miles, we never missed the July Indian Days in Browning.

Browning was a town of about a thousand Blackfeet residents and a handful of white businessmen. Except for the highway to Glacier National Park at the west end, all the roads leading to its main street were unpaved and rutted with potholes. The main street itself was a three-block strip of commercial establishments, some of which still bore the names of the traders who had arrived there seventy-five years before. J. H. Sherbourne's, the general merchandise store where you could buy hardware and furniture as well as groceries, stood near the Hagerty Hotel and the lumberyard. Interspersed between these larger concerns were a bank, a post office, the telephone switchboard (run by my mother's cousin and her husband), and several bars. Outside the Mint Pool Hall, the biggest and most popular of these old-style saloons, Blackfeet elders stood or sat in a row on a bench speaking Algonquian or, as people said then, "talking Injun." A trading post, a cafe, and several gas stations, one built in the shape of a tepee, lined the road to the park.

Off the main street stood a square of frame structures put up by the government to house the offices of the Bureau of Indian Affairs and the Blackfeet Tribal Council. The homes the Blackfeet themselves lived in were scattered on the unpaved streets that bordered the commercial district. These were mostly one-story frame houses, almost always in need of paint and repair, many with broken-down cars parked out in front. Children and dogs ran around in the dusty yards. The Blackfeet children and their mothers seldom appeared on the main street; the few native women we did see there were those who made their living as prostitutes to the white ranch hands who frequented the local bars.

The great circle camp of painted tepees that the Blackfeet put up every July, just outside the west end of town on the Browning fairgrounds, cut a sharp contrast to the seediness of the town. In the center of the camp, tribal leaders ceremonially raised an eight-sided medicine lodge of rawhide-tied cottonwood logs that were covered in the final stage of construction with a hundred sacred willows wrapped in clusters.

Accompanied by a steady beating of drums, the sacred dance to the Sun power began midday and continued into the night long after the crowd of spectators had dwindled. A tribal vow woman, who had fasted and prayed for three days while the men purified themselves with sweetgrass smoke in nearby hide-covered sweat houses, initiated the traditional ceremony and led the prayers of thanksgiving and renewal that punctuated the long day of mock battles and races, singing and dancing.

For this celebration of the tribe's holy medicine, young men donned the full ceremonial dress of their warrior ancestors and rode stallions decked in beaded martingales in a ceaseless parade past the assembled tribal leaders, whose war bonnets and head-dresses sprouted curved horns or streamed with eagle feathers that swept to the ground. Proudly clad in deerskin costumes heavy with native beadwork, women also rode, pulling their children in tra-vois attached to the saddles of their mounts.

The youths of the gathered tribes—young men who prided themselves on their skills in riding and roping—were also the fea-tured performers in the rodeo that preceded the Sun Dance cere-mony. In the chuck wagon race that opened the show, top-heavy wagons pulled by two-horse teams careened wildly around the fairgrounds arena to the spectators' cheers. It was an event as dan-gerous for the drivers as it looked from the stands. Next were the riding contests—saddle-bronc and bareback, wild horse and bull. The contestants' mounts exploded from their bucking stalls into the open to the gasps and cheers of the crowd. Finally, after the calf roping and bulldogging (throwing a steer by seizing the horns and twisting its neck), came wild cow milking and wild horse saddling, crowd-pleasing contests in which a man depended less on his skill than his luck in the draw. If his cow was indeed wild, if the roper holding her was more than a little drunk, the contestant was un-likely to milk the required thimbleful in a cup within a winning time. With these side-slapping events, the rodeo came to its hi-larious, often chaotic, finale.

As we left the arena, even if we were worn out and nearly fever-ish with excitement from the rodeo spectacle, Donna and I still always begged our parents to stop for a few minutes at the tiny Museum of the Plains Indian on the edge of the fairgrounds. Lin-ing the walls of two simple rooms were cases of ancient pipes and feathered war bonnets, deerskin buskins and gloves and moccasins, beaded dresses and vests and belts. There were skinning and tanning implements of horn and bone, bows and arrowheads and spears—the tools of peace and war and survival—and, best of all, laid out in a diorama below the cases, miniature replicas of villages from a century before, battlefields and hunting grounds of prouder times. I would press my nose against the glass in wonder, unwilling to be pulled away no matter how long I had been allowed to linger.

My family's relationship with the Blackfeet was not limited to these events in which we were spectators. Like many local ranchers, my father leased land from individual Blackfeet owners in 40-, 80-, and 160-acre parcels that combined to make up much of the pasturage on the north range. When he went into Browning to renegotiate these contracts—the leases came up separately at staggered renewal times—he worked not with the Indian owners themselves but with Charlie Gerard, a member of the tribe who oversaw its brokerage at the Blackfeet Agency. For an hour or so, the two men would pore over the rolled sectional maps that Charlie pulled out to determine which owners were due to be notified of renewals.

Out on the street again, the irony of a white man's easy access to cheap and plentiful land didn't escape my father as he walked past the poor descendants of the proud lords of the Plains. His method of telling me and, I suppose, himself as well about the subtle tension that existed between the Blackfeet and the white ranchers who profited from their current lot was to remind me of the rock ledge he had once pointed out to me up the river from the ranch. There in the sandstone, an Indian had scratched his declaration: "June 15, 1894. James White Calf. This is my ranch."

Another, more personal nexus existed between my father and the Indian crew who came to the ranch to help during haying every summer—always Charlie Cree Medicine and Willie Champlain

James White Calf's sandstone deed

and James Spotted Eagle, along with two or three of their neighbors or friends. Whenever my father went into Browning to renew leases during the winter or spring, he stopped first at the hotel to change a twenty-dollar bill into silver dollars, which he handed out a few at a time to these men, who shyly whispered, "Bill," or simply fell silently in step beside him as he passed the Mint Pool Hall. If the men had been drinking, they would be less reserved and leave backslapping and glad-handing with loud promises—"Be out to work it off, Bill," and "Don't worry, whenever you need me." And, sure enough, in early July, just about the time my father and Jimmy had finished repairing and greasing the mowers and making sure there were plenty of replacement sickles on hand and were getting ready to hitch up the horses (one team to mow, another to rake, and two to haul the hay to the stacks), Charlie would ride down to the ranch with his band of hayers.

Charlie Cree Medicine was a tall, sharp-featured man with a

straight back and the long muscles of a distance runner. His face—darker than ours but even after hours in the sun not as bronzed as those of many of his fellow Blackfeet—was pitted from childhood acne, and his hair was jet black, coarse and straight. Like almost all the members of his tribe, he had large, bulbous earlobes. Retiring, soft-spoken, and methodical, he was the man the hayers took their directions from, and he got along well with my father.

Charlie ran the mower himself, always moving across the fields clockwise, and he directed James Spotted Eagle when he came through a day or two later with the rake. The mower was low to the ground and heavy, with an iron frame and wheels and even iron seats. A wooden tongue hitched at the rear extended forward the length of the horses and was fastened onto each collar of the team. A sickle, driven by gears modulated to match its speed to the pace of the horses, moved back and forth cutting the hay. When Charlie spotted a rock or a nest of birds or rabbits in his path, he could raise the blade with a stirrup pedal on the right side of the seat.

We mowed the native grasses and wild clover and timothy that grew along the river and in the coulees on the east range. When the first settlers arrived here, these untouched fields had been chest high, almost too thick to walk through. We also mowed one field of alfalfa that we cultivated on the opposite bank. My favorite part of haying was the day or so we spent in the alfalfa field, because it was populated at this time of year by dozens of small creatures—rabbits and birds and mice. My sister and I came across a slaughtered nest of baby rabbits there one summer. After that, until I was old enough to be included as a member of the haying crew, I would run with her back and forth ahead of Charlie's mower to alert any small creatures nesting there to the havoc heading toward them.

The rake was one piece of equipment simple enough for me to operate, and by the time I was nine, I routinely took it over when

James Spotted Eagle went off for his lunch break or was helping out on the haystack. On these occasions, my father hooked up the gentlest team to this wide, iron-framed machine with its curved sharpened rods that were raised and lowered to release the hay into neat windrows. With the horses' reins tied to the seat in a loop knot, my hands were free to hold on as I slid a quarter way off to reach the pedal and trip the rake through its cycles.

After the hay had cured in windrows for a few days, it was time to bring the wagons out into the fields. The men used four-point forks to pitch the hay onto a net that covered the floor of the wagon bed. When the wagon was nearly full, one of the men would climb up and top off the load with a few final forkfuls. Once loaded, we could clamber on board for a ride to the stack, where Willie Chaplain would direct a boom that lifted the net full of hay from the wagon and dropped it onto stacks shaped like huge loaves of bread.

Lying back in the soft hay, I could look down on the muscles moving in the backs and shoulders of the horses, watch their heads swinging rhythmically from side to side. I would breathe in the sweet aroma of alfalfa or the stronger, almost musky tang of the dusty grasses from the range meadows and remove a sticky spine of Canadian thistle from my hand. As the wagon rolled over the washboard path on its way to the stack, I would close my eyes and read a tactile map of the terrain.

Horses

My father kept more horses than he needed or could reasonably use—a various band of twenty or so that included four or five work teams, half a dozen riding mounts, a colt or two, a cantankerous Shetland pony, and several old dobbins he couldn't bring himself to send off to the glue factory. He never let anyone who worked or rode these animals mistreat them; if he discovered a mouth raw from roughly jerked reins or a sore worn by a carelessly fit saddle, whoever was responsible received a quick reprimand. Although I don't remember anyone ever accusing Dad of being sentimental about animals, he treated horses, especially those he broke himself, with a tenderhearted mix of solicitude and enthusiasm that could only be called love.

Certainly there was nothing irrational in this affectionate appreciation. Nearly every important job on the ranch depended on these steady and hard-working animals. Horses pulled the fencing and the lambing wagons, the mower and the rake. They plowed the garden in late spring and hauled the hay across the fields and lifted it to the stack in the mid-July heat. Jimmy and the herders rode horseback to trail and herd the sheep, to round up and bring in the band from the range. On the coldest days of winter, a work team could be counted upon to trudge patiently along in front of the loaded sled from which we fed oil cake and hay to the sheep.

Like good sheepdogs, horses have to be trained to do ranch work. Breaking a workhorse is different from breaking one to ride, but the training starts out the same way. My father always began with a halter, gently leading the colt in a circle, occasionally laying a blanket or a leather strap across its back. This slow softening had to be continued for another two seasons before a horse was ready to be ridden, longer than that if it was to be worked. Whenever Dad saw a horse with a sway back, he grumbled that it had been saddled too soon or ridden by too heavy a rider. By the third year of breaking, a workhorse was ready to be fitted with bridle and collar and finally with full harness, but even then it still might not be heavily used on a team until the next season. The real test came when the novice was at last hitched up with a veteran—a stronger, bigger horse—to a wide-wheeled wagon. Coaxing the horse to accept both the wagon and a partner might well take a dozen hours spread over several days.

I remember a particularly nervous red sorrel whose skittishness my father had patiently suffered during three springs of breaking. When it was at last time to harness and hitch him to the training wagon, we all gathered in the open space between the house and the shed to watch. Jimmy and my father slowly led the harnessed horse out of his stall to the wagon. Although it took a while, the two of them managed to hitch him up without much trouble. Then, while Jimmy held the sorrel steady, my father climbed up onto the seat of the wagon and took hold of the reins and the trip ropes designed to give the trainer an extra edge of control.

Settled in the wagon, my father nodded to Jimmy that he was ready. The sorrel jerked forward, restrained more by his partner than by the reins, and the wagon bumped off. Under the unremitting pressure from the younger horse, the wagon gathered speed as it moved along past the snow fence out toward the road leading to the north range. Soon both horses had broken into a nervous gallop. The wagon disappeared over the hill like a vessel going to sea. When it reappeared half an hour later, both horses were dripping with sweat, but my father had somehow managed to regain control. Standing in the seat now, he yanked the trip ropes whenever the younger horse began to break stride. A month later, when he had finally given up on the sorrel as part of a work team, the horse became the chosen mount and companion of Andy. With this relaxed herder, the horse was pliant and docile, unless anyone else tried to ride him.

My sister and I shared my father's enthusiasm for horses, but for different reasons and in the child's way. Horses were first of all our constant companions and friends, the focus of our most entertaining summer pastimes and diversions, the gravitational center of our play. Donna always rode the big, gentle black gelding named Tony, while I climbed astride any horse not occupied at the moment—the Shetland, whose favorite bit of orneriness was to end his gallop at the gate in a short stop that sent me into a buffed-skin dismount, a workhorse, or one of the herders' mounts, but most often Lily, a plump, white mare.

The whole band of horses, except for a work team or two, wintered out on the range. During the coldest spells, they stayed on the hills close in, where they could depend on our hay and get water from the holes my father chopped in the ice-bound river. They roamed farther afield when the weather warmed up. Late in the spring, Donna and I would pester Dad to locate and bring them in so we could cut our riding horses along with the yearling colts from the herd. He usually gave in to our pleas on the first mild Sunday, and we would begin our search.

Intuition was our best guide in this open-range quest. Some years, the herd would have roamed ten or fifteen miles away, and although all of our horses bore my father's brand (A with a bowed crossbar), the composition of the herd would have changed since the previous fall, with wild stallions stealing mares to add to their harems. Their shaggy winter manes and subtle changes in color often made individuals difficult to spot. Still, the Shetland always stood out. After a winter on the range, he would look like a plump,

My sister Donna and I, summer of 1943

unkempt colt, his tail nearly touching the ground and shaggy locks covering his face. More often than not, it was the first sight of him that told us we had found our band.

The Shetland was distinguishable not only by his shagginess but also by his hooves, grown so long by spring that they curled up in front like Dutch skates. Trimming them was a major undertaking. That the pony could even get around on these hooves was a marvel, my father used to say. The task of trimming all the horses' hooves and shoeing those that would be worked and ridden always fell to Jimmy, who claimed his back wasn't bothered by the bending necessary to hold four dozen or more hooves against his chap-covered thigh. Some of the horses would come in half-lame, their hooves cracked or embedded with pebbles and dried mud. In a wing of the shed, Jimmy treated each horse in its turn, trimming and rasping, fitting and nailing on the iron shoes. Then, while he thinned their manes, front locks, and tails with a currycomb, my sister and I stood on harnessing benches and brushed the long winter hair from the riding horses' coats.

Many summer mornings right after breakfast, Donna and I would race down to the corral to get two mounts. As a rule, horses aren't as shy of children as they are of adults, but we still had to trick even Tony—oats rattled in a bucket, rope kept out of sight until the crucial moment—before we could lead him and one other horse into the shed to be bridled. If we planned a long ride, we might ask Jimmy to saddle them up before he started in on his work, but more often we simply rode bareback.

Mounting a saddleless horse on the open range can be problematic for a child rider. If we had to dismount, if we fell off or were thrown, we looked for a ledge above the river or a rock to stand on. Sometimes we made do with a steep hill; running at the horse from an incline, we could usually manage to leap onto its back. As we grew older, we more often regained a riding position by straddling the neck while the horse grazed and hanging on for dear life as it jerked up its head.

We had strict orders not to ride far from the ranch or to ford the river in high water, and, as a rule, we obeyed these commands. Since there were no working ranches or other kids nearby, we usually rode along the river, down as far as Jimmy's father's small place to the east, or in the other direction, up to the old Monroe place, where a house and shed and corral, abandoned long since, still stood on a rise above the opposite bank. On one summer excursion there, Donna and I spotted a beautiful brown-and-white pinto stallion on the bluff above us as we rode out of the water onto the bank. He had heard our horses crossing the river—his band had probably come down to lick the salt block near the abandoned shed or perhaps to graze in a nearby meadow—and had strutted out to have a look.

Our horses' ears perked up when the pinto whinnied to them, but they made no answer. Donna and I continued up to the road beyond the shed and onto the bluff. Alert to our approach, the stallion arched his head and began to gather his twenty-five or so mares and colts for retreat. Galloping and circling the flanks of the herd in tandem, the two of us managed to start the horses back toward the corral. But before we reached the bottom of the hill, the pinto regained control of his herd and raced ahead with them. After he had led the wild herd across the river, he turned to stare defiantly back at us, curious to see if we would follow him. This time, we did not.

One very hot afternoon not long after this encounter, Donna and I rode back to the old Monroe place, swatting the flies that were especially bothersome that summer from the necks of our horses as we went along. The pinto stallion and his herd had also returned and were gathered now in a shady corner of the corral, motionless except for their tails, which swished in concert against the flies. When the stallion caught sight of us, he began to pace nervously back and forth at the edge of the herd, finally moving toward the entrance of the corral. I closed the gate just before he reached it.

After the corralled horses had settled down, I took a rope from my saddle and the two of us climbed over the fence. The horses squealed and lifted their hind legs in half-hearted kicks, warning us not to come too close. With my rope I tracked a mare that had moved away from the rest for a while, then an attractive colt. As Donna and I moved around between the horses, they became more and more restless, their escalating panic finally driving us toward the gate. Once outside and back on my own mount, I unlatched the gate just before we escaped down the hill and back across the river. On the way home we agreed not to mention our stroll among the wild horses.

On the days Donna and I rode down the river, we usually stopped to see Jimmy's father, Shorty Dunbar, who lived three miles to the east in a tarpaper shack no larger than our kitchen and furnished as sparsely as a homesteader's. Outside, a lean-to protected the woodpile that supplied his stove, and his hobbled horse grazed nearby on the patch of grass the old man held as his grant from the reservation. Mr. Dunbar, as Donna and I always addressed him, was mostly Indian with a dash of Irish. Slightly stooped, he was smaller even than his diminutive son. He was over ninety and toothless and nearly deaf, but hopping around in his bib overalls and high, lace-up shoes, always busy with some project, he looked and acted like a much younger man.

I loved to watch the old man light up. Pulling out his folder of cigarette papers and putting one between his left thumb and index finger, he would jerk open the yellow strings of his sack of Bull Durham with his teeth and shake a shallow row of tobacco onto the paper. Then, after he stuffed the tobacco sack back into his pocket, he would raise his hands to his mouth to roll and lick the paper, bringing his right index finger across it to rub the seal and twist one end. A split second later, a wooden match (it seemed to appear by magic) would flare in a swipe across the right leg of his overalls. Finally, with the now lighted cigarette between his lips, he would pause one dramatic instant before he shook the match out and flicked it away, squinting after it to check the distance it traveled.

Mr. Dunbar admired my mother, never failing to inform me whenever we met, "Your mother is a beautiful woman." The year I was nine he trapped gophers for months, skinning them and nailing the pelts up to dry on a wall of the shack, for a coat he planned to make for her. Every time we rode in to see him that summer, he took us outside to admire the pelts and listen to his elaborate description of the design he had in mind for the coat. But Mr. Dunbar fell sick that fall and died before he could finish his project. The next summer when we rode down to his place, the pelts, shriveled now, were still hanging on the side of the deserted shack. We missed the old man.

When other families visited my parents, we would round up a horse for every child who could ride; those who couldn't rode double. Once when the two Thomas children had stopped in for the day with their parents, Donna and I had brought out Tony, Lily, and the Shetland, but we were still one horse short. Andy had left the red sorrel behind when he went to the mountains that year to save him from the deer flies there, and I decided to ride him myself, with an Indian bridle. I tied one loop of wool twine through the horse's mouth and around his lower jaw, attached two longer strands to it for reins, mounted bareback without a problem, and started out up the road. But, as the other horses came alongside us, the sorrel began to prance and thrust his head forward until he had so loosened the reins that I couldn't control him with the makeshift bridle. When one of the reins came free, the horse suddenly took his head in a full-stride run up the hill.

The sorrel was faster by half than any horse I had ever ridden. As he circled the hill and raced back down the west side toward the snow fence, I clung to his mane and scissored my legs into his ribs, braced for the sudden stop I knew would pitch me over his head. But instead of pulling up short at the six-foot fence, the horse leapt it with the grace of a deer. I left his back at the crest of his jump, for a second or two actually airborne beside him. The horse and I hit the ground at the same time, both of us glad that the ride was over. As I lay on the ground, amazed that I didn't hurt more than I did, the sorrel stood over me and waited for me to get to my feet. When I finally managed to pull myself up—nothing seemed to be broken— I removed the loop from his jaw and together we ambled along the same way I had seen him dozens of times with Andy when they trailed the sheep together. Despite this demonstration of the sorrel's gentler side, I decided not to ride any more that day.

Woman's Work

I've always suspected that what weighed down my mother's spirits during the first year she and my father lived on the ranch, the thing that kept her close to tears and more than once caused her to faint dangerously near to the stove, was not the drudgery of a ranch wife's life (although, heaven knows, there was plenty of that) but simple loneliness. She had grown up with four sisters on the edge of one little town or another, and even in the early years of her marriage she had been surrounded by other people on the ranches where she and my father hired on together. Now she found herself isolated with her husband and children, cut off for months at a time not just from her family but also from the companionship of other women. Early in 1942, when she was pregnant again and my father decided that someone should be brought in to assist her in the house, she must have been as glad for the company as she was for the help.

For a year or so, the women came and went. They were hired to assist my mother with the housework and to take over some of the routine cooking. A couple of them turned out to be alcoholics and had to be sent on their way even though they were good workers. Of those who were sober, one was so inept she botched every task she was put to, charring the food and scorching the clothes, but she tried so hard that Mother kept her on for a while, to reward her dogged efforts, I suppose. When another appeared in a housecoat to cook the men's breakfast on her first morning with us, she was sent back to town that same day.

I can remember a very young Indian woman named Wanda who came in one summer from Browning to work during shearing. My mother was stocking the cookhouse when Wanda arrived, so she sent her up to the house with instructions to clean. When Mother appeared an hour or so later to see how the new helper was getting along, she found that the girl had stripped the living room—even the curtains had been taken down—and was scrubbing the walls. Wanda stayed. At the end of this sequence of temporary workers, sometime early in the spring of 1944, Ida Belgrade appeared at our door to fill the household position once and for all.

Although Ida was a likely enough candidate to be my mother's permanent right hand in the house, she was not the person one might have predicted to become her companion and friend as well. Already Mother's senior by half a dozen years, with thinning hair tied up in a scarf and false teeth she clicked back into place as she talked, she looked, and acted too, much older than her age. Nervously lighting one cigarette from another (even after hours submerged in hot water, the tips of her fingers still showed the yellow stains), she was standoffish with Jimmy and the other men, even with my father. Fastidious about her work and efficient, she brooked no nonsense. And, unlike my mother, she had been around. But the two women worked well together and soon came to trust each other. From the early days of their association, they shared their women's concerns and secrets along with the housework.

Even in the mid-1940s, running the house on a ranch was more drudgery than not, primarily for the lack of such simple conveniences as hot water and dependable electricity, or natural gas for a stove. But on our place, the wind charger delivered the power for running water and made a refrigerator and a washing machine possible as well. A gravity tank in the attic supplied enough cold water to flush a toilet and fill a bathtub, undisputed luxuries in those days. We still used wood in the kitchen stove in the summer, burning coal in the winter, when it stayed lighted all day. One of my early duties was to load a metal scrub pail with the coal chunks or sticks of wood that fueled this cast-iron behemoth and drag it from the woodshed up onto the porch. A kerosene stove in the dining room heated the rest of the house, but whole rooms upstairs had to be closed off during the coldest months.

The endless preparation of meals began every morning with the kindling of the kitchen stove before daybreak for six-o'clock breakfast and ended with the dinner dishes around seven in the evening. While the stove was firing up, my mother or Ida mixed the batter for pancakes, which they served to the men with eggs and bacon or occasionally sausage, all cooked in oversized cast-iron skillets too heavy to lift with one hand, along with hot cereal and dried prunes or apricots that had soaked overnight.

The men liked thick pancakes, ones that "stuck with you for a while," but I preferred the airier, crepelike versions I had eaten in town and would wait until my mother had finished everyone else's order before begging her to make mine "the thin way." I seldom ate the oatmeal or Cream of Wheat because, like my sisters, I hated the curdled taste of canned milk (fresh milk went bad too quickly, my mother thought). Sometimes I would make an exception for corn flakes or Shredded Wheat so I could send in for a Captain Midnight decoder ring or unearth the adventure cards tucked between the layers of biscuits.

Throughout these early morning meals, cup after cup of coffee was poured scalding hot from a huge gray- and black-speckled enamel pot that boiled away on the back of the stove. Some of the men drank theirs in ritualistic styles, which I watched with some interest. Lifting the cup to his mouth, one would slurp a few drops, pull back from the hot liquid for an instant, then move in for another short sip. He never returned the cup to its saucer until he had carried out half a dozen of these abridged attempts. Andy's approach was not only the most elaborate but also the most offensive to my mother's sensibilities. After pouring an ounce or two from his cup into the saucer and pushing back his chair from the table, he would lean down to blow across the coffee until it had reached the desired temperature. Then he would draw the liquid over the edge of the saucer in a single windy slurp. At my mother's insistence, my father spoke privately to Andy; after that he drank his coffee sitting up like everyone else.

A good breakfast in a warm kitchen put everyone at the table in high spirits. Only when my mother served toast instead of pancakes did anyone grumble. The bread was toasted on the open wood fire, so it always carried the burnt taste of charcoal. If there had to be a substitution, Jimmy would protest, it should be cinnamon rolls. Throughout the meal, the men talked loudly, laughing and occasionally playing a little joke on the cook. ("Look what I found in my eggs!") My mother enjoyed her revenge for these pranks one April Fools' Day, when she baked paper disks between layers of batter to create pancakes that pulled apart in ragged pieces around their slippery hidden centers when the men tried to cut them.

As soon as Mother and Ida had washed the breakfast dishes and hung their recycled flour-sack towels up to dry, they would begin baking bread and pie crusts or cookies or a cake for the next few meals. Unless it was a wash day, this time and the hour or so after lunch were the most relaxed of their day. The two women drank coffee and chatted while they worked, growing quiet when it was time for Ida's favorite radio program, *My Gal Sunday*. If the supper menu included chicken fried in lard, my mother would dip feathered hens my father had killed that morning into boiling water and then pluck them. The kitchen would reek of burnt down after she seared the last fuzz from the birds' skin.

Since my mother believed that hot water was an absolute requisite to getting things clean, washing clothes was almost a full day's work. The women heated the ten gallons required for each load in the Easy in a copper tub on the back of the stove. Except on the coldest days, the washing was hung outside. Each pillowcase and tablecloth and shirt was stiff when it was taken down or, if it was still damp, it was draped over a wooden rack inside to dry for another hour or two. Even though Monday was officially wash day, my mother seemed to be perpetually pinning or unpinning clothes from the line where a cotton bag of wooden clothes pegs always hung.

My mother ironed everything, of course, even sheets and doilies and underwear. But first she dipped her own blouses and Donna's dresses in cooking pots of hot starch before wringing them a second time, and she sprinkled every piece of laundry by hand. Rolled up in tight bundles, the clean clothes waited beneath a damp towel in an apple basket that I'm sure was never empty. Whenever either woman had a free moment, she would set up the ironing board and press a few items. Only when the wind hadn't blown for a while did they drag out the heavy iron relics that were heated on the stove; most of the time, the wind charger supplied enough power for the electric iron.

Unless it was very cold, Donna and I amused ourselves outside during the day, and with the whole ranch for a playground we usually found something to do without getting into trouble. But my mother still worried, especially if my father and Jimmy were away, and tried to keep an eye on us from the kitchen while she worked. She was most apprehensive that we might be stepped on by a horse or butted by one of the rams kept behind the shed for fall breeding. Nevertheless, we played with the horses and even ventured on occasion into the rams' pen, which couldn't be seen from her window. One exciting stunt my sister and I enjoyed was to pull the rams' feeding trough away from the wall so that a pitched battle between butting heads would break out when the animals ate from both sides.

The only ranch animal I was ever wary of was a particularly testy gobbler, which came rushing out, its huge wings flapping, to peck at my face and arms whenever I passed the henhouse the summer I was eight.

Sometimes when she was especially busy, Mother would put Donna and me in charge of our baby sister, warning us to watch her carefully and to stay close to the house. Even as a toddler, Joleen would agree to be hoisted up on the Shetland, like a city child at the fair, but she much preferred to be pulled around the yard in her old baby buggy, which we hooked up to Tony's saddle horn with a rope. When my mother decided horse-drawn rides in this tipsy vehicle were too dangerous and outlawed them, we hooked Tony up to the handle of a scoop shovel, where the girls took turns riding while I sat on the horse. I liked to start these rides off with such a jolt the passenger stayed put as the shovel suddenly slid away.

Although my mother's worries about our hurting ourselves around horses and rams were probably justified, our only close call with disaster involved a machine rather than an animal. The three of us had been playing among the oil cake sacks in the granary, where my father also kept his three outboard motors bolted to a board between two of the beams. When the hide-and-seek amusement we had set up for the toddler began to bore us, I decided to see if I could start the little trolling engine. Climbing up on an oil drum, I wound the rope around the starter pulley and gave it a yank. After sputtering along for a moment, the engine coughed off. Still, we were so pleased with my success that Donna followed me up near the oil drum when I announced I was going to try the big motor.

Donna stood next to me while Joleen, her head tilted up and her hands tucked into the front of her overalls, watched earnestly from in front of the propeller. Starting this larger engine was more of a challenge, and after two hard jerks on the rope I had managed to produce only a cough or two and a puff of blue smoke. I rewound the rope and gave a third mighty yank, falling off the barrel when the engine came alive. Donna screamed out in alarm and Joleen jumped back from the whirling propeller. Without water to keep it cool, the engine was already smoking by the time I climbed back up onto the oil drum. Desperately fumbling with knobs and valves, I finally brought the whining full throttle to a stop with a rubber grip on the steering column.

Blue smoke and hot engine fumes filled the room. Donna and I knew this had been a serious transgression: Joleen had barely escaped the propeller's blades and my father never started these engines without putting them in water first. We quickly opened all the granary doors, except those facing the house, and beat the air with empty oil cake sacks to clear the fumes. Although we admonished each other and Joleen not to mention this adventure, I continued to worry about being found out for days afterward and watched nervously for some malfunction when my father started the big motor at Two Medicine Lake two Sundays later.

Even when the ranch hands left the house every evening after dinner, the women still had a few tasks left before they too could relax. While Ida washed the dishes, my mother would draw a tub of water from the gravity tank in the attic, hauling another few buckets from the stove to make it tolerably warm. Then, one after another, my younger sister always first, the three of us took our baths. After the last had finished, Ida would mop the kitchen floor with the gray bath water and retire to her room off the kitchen.

Before we were put to bed, we were allowed to play for an hour in the living room while my mother crocheted or knitted on the couch and my father read a magazine in his overstuffed chair next to the cabinet radio. My parents didn't own many books, only a few Zane Grey westerns and, of course, *The Big Sky* by A. B. Guthrie Jr., whose father had been my mother's high school principal in Choteau. Sometimes Dad would soak his feet in a basin while he read a magazine; the heavy White boots he wore all day were durable and suited to his work, but they couldn't have been comfortable. After a while, he would join the three of us on the floor to give the baby a ride on his back and roughhouse with Donna and me.

To ensure good reception from stations farther away than KFBB in Great Falls, my father had run a radio cable to the house from a pole he put up at the top of the bluff. On Friday nights, he tuned in the Gillette Cavalcade of Sports to hear the blow-by-blows of bouts featuring Joe Louis and Billy Conn and Jersey Joe Walcott. I can still hear the resonant, high-pitched voice that opened these broadcasts: "This is Don Dunphy, coming to you from Madison Square Garden." I also liked to listen to "The Shadow," with its baleful narrator ("Who knows what evil lurks in the hearts of men? The Shadow knows!") and "The Whistler" and "Inner Sanctum," with its creaking door, and Donna and I never missed "Let's Pretend" on Saturday mornings. Interrupting our play outside to sit up close to the round center speaker of the Philco, we strained to catch every word of the tales spun out in the actors' voices—Blue Beard and Snow White and Rose Red and The Juniper Tree.

But most nights the Philco was turned off after the early evening news unless there had been a major development on some front of the war. When the Philippines fell, when Germany was defeated in North Africa, when Patton and Montgomery landed in Italy, during the night bombings of London and the Normandy invasion, the adult conversation would stop every time the news announcer's voice broke through the static. When President Roosevelt died in the spring of 1945, the radio ran for days.

At eight, my mother would lay aside her needles and yarn and take us in to bed. After she led us in a quick recital of "Now I Lay Me Down To Sleep," the prayer she had embroidered and hung in a frame over our beds, and closed our door behind her, we would make just enough noise that she would send my father back in to quiet us down. His appearance in the doorway of our room would set off another few minutes of hilarity, which sometimes included a pillow fight or a story and always wound down with Dad's own irreverent version of our prayer. The line of this parody I liked best was "a bag of peanuts at my feet." Finally, he would announce: "I mean it now; time to settle down." Almost as soon as he had closed our door again, I would be asleep.

Vacation

Late on a Saturday afternoon soon after shearing, and three or four other times between the middle of June and the first week of August, my father would stride into the kitchen to announce without prelude or warning, "Time to go to the park." This news always propelled my mother into a flurry of food preparation. As she flew around the kitchen, flouring pieces of chicken and throwing potatoes into a pot to boil, she would mutter that she might have been given a little more notice, but no one ever believed she was unhappy. Driving up to Glacier Park for the day with a picnic basket in the trunk and the boat hitched behind was an outing we all loved.

By 8:00 the next morning, we would be on our way. My parents sat up front smoking, the side vents of the Ford coupe slanted open so the wind didn't whip into our faces. In the backseat with our baby sister perched between us, Donna and I read comic books for the first dozen miles or so. When we tired or ran out of these, we vied in calling out the makes of passing cars or teased Joleen until she started to fuss and Mother had to take her up front. Half a dozen miles west of Browning, where the road leaves the plains to wind on between groves of willow and aspen, hemlock and red fir, ponderosa and tamarack, we would quiet down and simply look out the windows.

We usually stopped to stretch our legs in East Glacier, the official entrance to Glacier National Park. My mother liked to stroll a few minutes along the double rows of formal gardens planted with all the flowers from Shakespeare, which ran between the wood frame train station and East Glacier Lodge, both built by the Great Northern Railroad early in the century to attract tourists from the

East. On the station platform there were always three or four Blackfeet men in ceremonial dress, hired by the railroad to "act native" while they greeted incoming passengers.

Donna and I would race to the lodge, where the lobby was as big as a cathedral, its timbered ceiling suspended on giant firs an amazing three stories above us. A stuffed mountain goat stood in a glass case just outside the cavernous dining room, which we always peeked into before we ran outside again. In our own living room at home, we had a miniature wooden replica of this very goat, one of hundreds carved by John L. Clarke, the deaf grandson of a famous Blackfeet leader, Chief Stands Alone.

Winding north from East Glacier on the two-lane highway gouged out of limestone toward our destination at Two Medicine, a dramatic vista appeared at every bend in the road—deep valleys stretching out between cliffs and spires, streams boiling with pale green glacial runoff, Trick Falls with its double gushing spouts, Rising Wolf and Never Laughs Mountain. Not just grander, they were brighter, prettier too, than the miniature reproductions of them on the postcards sold back at the lodge. But there was always more than scenic excitement on this leg of the trip. As the coupe crawled along in a string of cars—on summer Sundays, the park would be crowded with visitors—Donna and I would watch for the bears.

Along this stretch of highway, the black bears and brown bears (even then, seldom a grizzly) that showed up alongside the road looking for food, perhaps for attention, sometimes outnumbered the people. Except for an occasional "Don't Feed Wild Animals" sign, the Park Service didn't bother much about warnings in those days. Tourists stopped their cars to gawk and take pictures. An irascible adult bear would push its head through the open window of a vehicle stalled in the traffic; a cub in search of food might try to scramble into the backseat of a car parked on the shoulder.

Although my sisters and I loved to watch this hullabaloo, my father took a dimmer view of the tourists' lack of prudence. In his days running pack horses for the Forest Service, he had had a territorial encounter or two with an irritable mother bear and had heard of more than a few outright attacks. Trapped in the line of slow-moving cars, he was impatient to be on his way, apprehensive perhaps not so much about the danger as the inevitable paw scratches on the doors of the coupe.

After twelve miles, we always turned off the highway onto the road leading to the Two Medicine campgrounds below Cut Bank Pass, the high place where our river began. A century or more before, the Blackfeet who held this valley had been driven out by white prospectors, forced in the end officially to cede all their mountain territories when the area became part of the national park. The lakes at Two Medicine took their name not from their number (there were actually three separate bodies of water carved out in a chain by the glacier) but from two Blackfeet clans who once quarreled over the surrounding territory and finally settled their differences by assigning the middle lake to one group while the other camped and fished and made medicine at the lower lake.

Pulling into the picnic grounds beside the middle lake at Two Medicine, we would meet up with my father's best friend, Wilfred Nadeau, and his family. The Nadeaus were easy to spot because they drove a four-door Cadillac sedan and pulled a mahogany boat identical to ours—a covered-bow, plank-seated model with "Johnson Seahorse" stamped on the silver motor. While our mothers collected the babies and picnic baskets from the cars, Donna and I would race with Gary and Rebba Jo, the older Nadeau children who were our age, to claim our favorite tables in the sunny clearing near the place where the river flowed out of the lake. Inseparable when it was time to relax, my father and Wilfred would launch the boats and yell at us to hurry so they could get on to their favorite fishing spot at the far end of the lake.

Although we children went along just for the fast ride up the lake, the two men feigned a sincere interest in the fish. They never caught much. The falls below kept native fish from migrating into the lake, which itself was halfheartedly stocked. Nevertheless, the two of them trolled away the late morning, pulling shiny red and green spinners from their tackle boxes or, if they had decided to go after "the big ones," chains of cowbells and oversized plastic lures that magnified live minnows inside them. Around one, when everyone was hungry and ready for a break, we would race the twin boats back down the middle of the lake.

When we returned to the grounds, Mother and Gladys Nadeau would have set out our picnic. My mother always brought fried chicken and potato salad, carrot sticks and sliced fruit and chocolate cake, but Gladys's basket often yielded more exotic fare— smoked herring or crab salad, imported crackers in a China blue tin, perhaps even a bottle of wine. After lunch, while the children skipped flat rocks across the smooth surface of the lake, the adults would sit for a while in the shade and talk politics.

My father was a Democrat, but like many Montanans of those times he was sometimes ambivalent about Roosevelt's policies. Certainly he liked the way the president was handling the war effort, and he was grateful for the low-interest loans offered through the Farm Credit Administration and for the cooperative grazing rights on public lands made possible by the Taylor Act. Still, he was critical of what he and Wilfred referred to as make-work programs—the WPA and parts of the new Social Security Act, for example. Like many Westerners who were profiting from the New Deal and the revived economy, he believed nonetheless in individualism and self-reliance, and he worried that some of the benefits the government was now providing were undermining people's faith in the values that had ensured their survival in hard times.

As a rule, Gary and I declined our fathers' invitation to rejoin them in the boats. Unlike stream fishing, trolling was a boring business, I thought. Instead, we would find something else to do. We tracked the river half a mile into the trees or wandered through the picnic grounds with the girls to spy on other picnickers—a carful of nuns out for the afternoon, a troop of uniformed Boy Scouts on a nature hike, three city children trying to feed their sandwiches to the chipmunks around the garbage bins.

By six, or earlier if an afternoon wind had cut the fishing short, we were on our way home. With Joleen sprawled asleep across our laps, Donna and I would be quiet now, tired out with play, drowsy from the mountain air. For a few miles we looked out the windows where the trees flashed by, then fell asleep ourselves to the drone of the radio before we reached the turnoff onto the plains.

For our annual vacation the first week of August, we always went to Swan Lake, in the resort area a few miles south of Kalispell. The tree-covered mountains there were less majestic than those in Glacier Park, gently sloping down from the Swan Range, which framed the east side of the lake into wide meadows. There ranchers raised cattle mostly, and mowed hay to feed them. A three-hour drive from the ranch with the boat in tow, it was about as far away from home as we ever went.

Every year we rented the same cabin, an unpainted frame affair with two pine-paneled rooms and a tiny kitchen in a cluster of ten or so scattered across a wooded slope between the sign at the edge of the highway ("Patterson's Housekeeping Cottages") and the gravel beach. Just a few feet from our porch was a little wooden arch of a bridge that a creek trickled under on its way down to the lake. The Christmas card the Pattersons sent us each December

With Dad at Swan Lake, summer of 1946

invariably featured a shot of this accommodation in the photograph pasted on the front.

At Swan Lake, my father got serious about fishing. Besides his
five-horse Johnson motor for trolling the shoreline close to the
cabin, he brought along a more powerful Evenrude, which whisked
us up and down the lake to the most remote fish haunts. By six
every morning, all of us, even Mother and Joleen, would be on the
dock, loading up gear for a daylong excursion; half an hour later
our boat would be passing back and forth in the funnel current
where the Swan River flows into the lake at the south end.

My mother would lie back lazily against the cushions in the
bow. She found trolling relaxing but rarely bothered with pole or
line, and as far as I can remember, she almost never caught a fish. I,
on the other hand, was expected to participate more actively.
Daydreaming at the end of my pole, I would gaze up at the sky,
follow the slow-motion flight of an osprey across the lake to its nest

at the top of a nearby lodgepole. Never have I been wired with whatever telepathic sense it is that twitches just before the line does, but my father was always alert to the critical moment. "Pay attention, now," he would admonish me, "you're about to get a strike."

In spite of our restlessness, my father generally caught a respectable number of fish by late morning. Then he would turn the boat out into the lake again and head it toward the bays at the northeastern end, where the manicured lawns of a dozen large houses swept down to the water. No one ever seemed to be at home at these palatial vacation spreads, which my mother admired and always referred to as "estates." After we had tied up at one of the docks and eaten our lunch on the grass there, we might putt back down the unsettled western shore of the lake, pulling in here and there at an overgrown cove to explore one or another of the little creeks that ran down the banks and reminded my father of the streams around Bynum, where he had fished as a boy. It was on one of these expeditions, during the August when I was nine, that we first came across what the people in my family have called ever since "the lost cabin."

Following a creek that fed into the lake close to the remains of a washed-up dock, we had trudged half a mile through heavy brush along the bank that afternoon when the undergrowth thinned out at the edge of a clearing. In the center of this tree-framed open space we saw a splendid little body of water, perhaps three hundred feet long and half as broad—a miniature lake, in fact—created by a heavy-timber and wire mesh dam on the dirt levee at one end. A green metal rowboat was tied up at a makeshift dock on one side, and above it on a little rise stood a log cabin not much bigger than a tree house.

My sister and I scrambled up the slope and onto the sagging porch of the cabin. Looking in through the window beside the door at a single, plank-floored room, we could see everything there was to see: a woodstove in one corner, a bed against the wall, a table and chair. No one was at home, and something about the room suggested that no one had been there for some time, but it looked as if whoever lived there had started to make bread. A sifter and a can of lard were out on the table, and flour was strewn over the oilcloth cover they rested on. Had the owner been called away suddenly by some urgent business, we wondered, or perhaps been struck down and later carried away?

Our speculations were interrupted by my father's calls to us from the dock. When we caught up with him, he was wearing an expression of pure delight. Leaning over the water, he pointed out to us what he had descried there twelve feet below. The bottom of the little lake was black with trout.

My father and I untied the boat and pushed off across the stream current into the center of the water. There, we cast lines tied with royal coachman flies to trout that struck the instant our hooks hit the water. We pulled in one or two apiece, twelve-inch rainbows that flopped heavily against the metal floorboards. Then the fish, spooked either by our noisy glee or the midday sun or both, stopped biting altogether.

The two of us returned alone to challenge the trout at the hidden lake when the sun was lower the next afternoon, and once again after that before the end of our week at Swan. We fished from the shore near the dock on these occasions, for a few giddy minutes each time reeling in one after another of the shimmering fish, gray-blue-green iridescences above the clean white bellies. But both times the canny trout again retreated from our hooks all at once, as if responding to some unheard alarm.

I've returned to Swan Lake twice as an adult, each time on a sentimental journey to show a child the mysterious lost cabin of our family stories. Strangely enough, of all the local people I talked to on these visits, only one old man who had lived in the area all his life had ever heard of the tiny house with its own trout lake, and even he had never actually seen the spot. Before the war, he told me, a caretaker to one of the large houses at the end of the lake was said to have built himself a cabin on the unsettled western shore, hauling all the lumber in by boat. He was sure the caretaker had died years before—how many he couldn't say—and what had happened to his little house and the lake, he didn't know.

Even without directions from the locals, finding the cabin was easy enough on the first visit with my wife, Ann, and our three-year-old daughter, Kerstin. The western shoreline of Swan Lake had not altered in the twenty-five years or so since I'd been there, and although no remnant of the washed-up dock remained, in our rented outboard I found the stream to lead us there in the place where I thought it must be.

Nothing had changed. There was the lake, still dammed at one end, with dozens of trout hovering near the bottom in the green water around the dock. There was the metal boat, rustier now than I remembered but clearly the same one, tied to the dock where my father and I had left it, and above it on the rise, the deserted cabin.

Kerstin, even then often more delighted with fable than reality, was less amazed by this scene than her mother or I. Perhaps the setting she had pictured from my stories was more otherworldly than the one she now stood in, or perhaps the reality was unremarkable precisely because it matched her vision of it. Whatever the case, she was still enchanted enough by the old boat to allow herself to be seated in it next to me and pushed off from the dock. But the rusty craft began at once to take on water and we were forced to return to the landing. I cast from the shore for a while in the midday sun, but the fish could see me and stayed away from my line.

I am never easily deterred where there are trout to be caught, so the next day we returned to the hidden lake, this time lugging an oversized inner tube. Entering the water where it was shallowest, I paddled toward the center until my feet no longer touched bottom, and I began to cast. This time the trout could hardly wait for my flies, and I reeled in one fish after another until I looked up to Ann's warning cries to see the wake of an adult beaver that was swimming aggressively in my direction.

With the beaver following like a miniature submarine, I paddled back to safety, swatting the water with my rod in its direction. As soon as my feet hit the muddy bottom, the beaver, satisfied that it had reclaimed its territory, circled back toward the far end of the lake. For the rest of the afternoon, I settled for fishing from the shore with my wife. Spin casting short of the spot I had reached in my inner tube, we caught a few more trout, but for the first time my skills suggested perhaps I had been in the city too long.

On my second return to Swan Lake twenty years later, I brought my teenaged son, William. This time, the enchanted place of my childhood was more elusive. Setting out in another rented outboard, I lost control of the boat almost before we had cleared the dock, nearly running it aground on the rocks surrounding the cove. We putted up and down the western side of Swan for well over an hour, but the shoreline had been altered by the intervening winters, and none of the five or six creeks I spotted from the boat matched the decaying images of my mental map. Finally, more in response to Will's pleas that we abandon the search than from any conviction, I pulled the boat into an overgrown cove where one of the larger streams trickled into the lake. "This is it," I announced with more confidence than I felt.

I tied up the outboard and started up the slope. The brush here was much thicker than I remembered it, and as I pushed along in front of Will through wild berry bushes that whipped back to sting my face and struggled to keep my footing on the soggy ground, I was fairly well convinced that I had chosen the wrong creek. After fifty yards or so of muttering, Will stopped short. "Dad, this is crazy," he called to me. "There's nothing up here." But, since the trees seemed to be thinning out, I kept going, and he trudged along unhappily, falling farther behind me but at least silent now.

Suddenly the clearing came into view ahead. "Hurry," I shouted back. "I told you it was here!" He caught up with me fast, still shaking his head in mock disgust but eager now to press on for verification.

As we walked across the remains of the dam at the end of the clearing, the first thing we saw was the bed of the little lake, empty now except for the creek bisecting it. A notice, posted on a tree by the Fish and Wildlife Service, explained the transformation. The dam had been opened and the lake drained as part of a fish-spawning renewal program. Fish like those that had blackened the water here were now free to migrate in and out of the lake.

But not everything had changed. The green metal boat I had climbed into, first with my father forty-five years before and then with my daughter, lay near the old dock, submerged in mud now and encrusted with rust, but still intact. On the rise above the lake bed, the cabin was still standing, its door hanging open. Squatters or hunters had evidently used this shelter; the decaying garbage of human campsites was strewn around inside and on the ground in front. The smell that met us when we entered the cabin suggested that bears and rodents had been there after them. "I'll be damned," Will said as he stood with me on the rotting porch, surveying the scene of a story he'd heard a hundred times.

When Will and I left the clearing to fetch his mother for a new look at the secret place, we stumbled onto an easier way back down, a path as smooth and open as a country lane just a few yards beyond the thatch of saplings and thorns and berry bushes that had obstructed our progress up the bank. On this stroll back to the boat, Will was full of excitement and talk.

As the outboard planed up Swan toward our lodgings on the west side, I began to muse, not for the first time, about the curious ways relationships between father and son work themselves out in each generation. My father and I danced along together in nearly wordless rhythms of work and play, each anticipating the other's actions, reading feelings by visceral signs. My son and I seldom work side by side, and when we do, we bump against each other like strangers. Yet, I am his confidant, his partner in a dance of words that binds us in an affection as strong as any I have known. Like his mother, Will has always been able to explain what he means and say what he feels. Even so, I sometimes long for him to read the meaning in my action, to sense my feelings in his gut.

Fall and Winter

Every mile is two in winter.

—GEORGE HERBERT

Boarding

Fall comes early to Montana, in crisp August mornings and chilly evenings that give summer notice. As late as October, a string of Indian summer days may hold back the cold, but well before Thanksgiving, winter moves into tenancy. Snow blows across the high plains east of the mountains, and in all of the nation only Fraser, Colorado, and West Yellowstone register more arctic temperatures. The cold presses down, crueler than the snow and more hazardous, lifting once or twice in the early months of the new year when a chinook wind rides through on the Pacific currents. During these unseasonable interludes, the air warms half a dozen degrees in a minute, and for the few days between storms, sheep forage for dead grass uncovered by the melting snow. But winter still holds possession when people reset their clocks to daylight saving time. I remember it as a time of truck heaters and cold feet.

September was a busy month for us. Hay and oil cake were trucked in to feed the new crop of lambs, and last year's yearlings had to be shipped off to Utah and Kentucky from the station at Blackfoot. We put antifreeze in the radiators of the trucks and the jeep and changed the oil in the engines to a lighter weight; we nailed protective sheeting over the windows in the houses and cleaned the stove flues. And, early in the month, my mother would take us into town to buy clothes and supplies for school—not just new shoes and jackets, pencils and notebooks, but also heavy gloves and overshoes, long underwear and leggings.

Late in the summer of the year Donna turned six, my parents had to settle the question of where to send her to school. Commuting every day from the ranch into town was impractical, and once winter had set in, often impossible. My father had attended the boarding school for boys at Mount St. Charles College in Helena, later renamed for its founder, Bishop John P. Carroll, the Indian missionary, who is remembered as the author of early treatises on the "heathen customs" of the Blackfeet. In 1942, when my father looked around for another Catholic boarding school, the nearest was St. Thomas Home for Children in Great Falls. Since there was just a year between my sister and me in age, my mother thought it would be nice if we were in the same grade. So it was decided that the two of us would start the first grade together there in September.

I was not quite five years old when I first stood with my parents and sister on the steps leading to the heavy oak door of St. Thomas Home. My earliest coherent recollection from childhood begins with this passage and ends nearly ten months later, with my return home for the summer. Although there are predictable gaps in these abiding memories, I can still call up dozens of details from this time, many of them involving a young nun, who was probably as lonely and homesick as I was. I had never been away from home before, never been separated from my mother and father, and in the beginning at least their absence felt like a permanent loss.

Donna was barely a year older than I. Growing up miles from town, apart from other children, we had been inseparable, our lives as fused as twins'. This close connection ended at the St. Thomas school. Only minutes after my parents had hugged us good-bye and disappeared down the hall, I watched with alarm as Donna was led off by a smiling nun to her dormitory. During the next months, I saw her mostly at meals, where she sat on the girls' side of the dining hall. I met up with her less often on the playground. As it turned out, I wouldn't see much of my father and mother during this year either. The demands of the ranch along with winter weather and the hundred-mile distance to Great Falls proved their plans to visit us every few weeks naively optimistic.

About thirty children slept in the dormitory I was assigned to, a mixed group of boys from five to eight years old, mostly orphans and foster placements, and a few boarders like me. There were also three nuns, who were in charge of the boys before and after school hours. The youngest of these women hurried across the room to welcome me when I was ushered into the dormitory that first afternoon. With her hands folded inside the bib of the long apron she wore over her habit, she bent down and smiled. I remember being surprised to see a strand or two of bright red hair peeking out from the edges of her starched wimple. Someone had told me that nuns didn't have hair. "What is your name, young man?" she asked.

Everyone at home had always called me Butch, but I was trying to act grown up or, short of that, older than I felt, so I supplied my more formal appellation. "Donald," I replied solemnly.

Later in the darkened dormitory, I lay awake on my cot, alert to the night sounds of the other children—rustlings and coughs, an occasional whisper. I missed my mother and our quiet bedtime prayer, my father's playful trips into our bedroom to settle us down. Instead of falling into the easy sleep that had always followed these nightly rituals, I kept a miserable watch. I had been abandoned, I thought, like an outgrown toy tossed into the attic.

When the young nun with the red hair floated down my aisle on her final bedtime rounds and heard my muffled crying, she leaned over and whispered, "You'd better sleep closer to me, Donald." After I had scrambled off my cot, she gathered up mattress and covers, and folding the ends of the bed in on the springs, nodded for me to follow her. In two silent trips, she collected all my things and then sandwiched my bed in next to her own at the far end of the room, where the three women slept behind a curtain drawn to secure them a little privacy.

Although I was sent down to the first-grade classroom the next morning after breakfast, I spent less than a week there at the desk beside my sister's. It must have been clear right away to whoever was in charge that at four, going on five, I was hardly ready to start school. Instead, I spent my days in the dormitory as the red-haired nun's companion, falling asleep in the cot next to hers after she kissed my forehead and gave my hand a reassuring pat each night. For the next nine months, I seldom left her side. Her name was Sister Theresa Joachim.

Some days, Sister Theresa and I cleaned the dormitory. My favorite chore was waxing the floor of the big playroom adjoining the room where we slept. After we had applied the wax, the two of us would run across the oak in wool-stockinged feet, from one end to quarter point, then, giggling, slide to the middle. When we had buffed off a quarter of this expanse, we reversed direction to do another.

Other days, she read me story after story and drew pictures of houses and trees and animals, which we colored together. "You can erase pencil mistakes like this," she demonstrated, rubbing her dampened finger tip lightly across an erring line. A cat magically appeared as she added just two pyramid ears and the curve of a tail to the pair of uneven circles she had told me how to draw, one above the other, on my paper. And I saw before she pointed it out to me that the cat was facing away from us.

When we arrived at the ranch for Christmas vacation, the first thing I caught sight of from the bridge was the charred hull of the sheep shed. My father had told us all about the fire on the drive from Great Falls—how it had started in some wood shavings, how quickly the old frame structure had been consumed by the flames. A pile of burlap sacks full of oil cake had smoldered for days, and everything stored inside except the horses' harnesses and tackle had been lost. The old gray tomcat that lived in the shed had been missing afterward; my parents assumed he had perished in the fire until he showed up in the yard the next week, tarred with scabs and missing his tail. Even though he had never been a house cat, he allowed my mother to take him inside, where for years he stayed on, his scorched hair giving place to patches of wrinkled skin.

I was ecstatic to be home again, the familiar winter rhythms of the ranch as exciting to me as Christmas. I went with my father when he cut holes in the ice for the horses and loaded straw to line the corrals. I tagged along on his trips to the near north range and on runs into town and rode in the truck every day while he fed hay and oil cake to the sheep. And I listened in closely when anyone spoke about spring. Tagging would begin in early March, and soon after that, the ewes would be brought in to lamb.

When I learned that I would be returning to Great Falls right after New Year's, I was crestfallen. It simply hadn't crossed my mind that my reprieve was not permanent, and even now I find this decision puzzling. I suppose I was sent along once again to keep my sister company. Or perhaps no one had informed my parents that I wasn't actually going to school. Whatever the case, my mother was pregnant that winter and feeling unwell; the first year on the ranch had been difficult for her. She must have imagined that if I were allowed to remain at home, my sister would want to stay too.

Returned to Great Falls, I spent the rest of the winter as I had the fall, more often than not in the dormitory with Sister Theresa. But I was less homesick now than I had been. My Aunt Cora, who lived nearby, appeared every other Sunday to take Donna and me to Gibson Park or the Historical Society Museum on the bus, and my father and mother made the trip to Great Falls more often. During these visits, my father told me all about the new sheep shed he was going to build. He had already hauled in the lumber from the mills in Kalispell and hired carpenters to help with construction. I longed to be part of all this excitement.

I don't remember the morning we left Great Falls for good, nor, strangely enough, do I recall saying good-bye to Sister Theresa, although that parting must have been melancholy for us both. Well into my high school years she continued to send me nature stamps and St. Christopher medals, tucked inside letters I always tried to answer. But I can call up a vivid memory from later in that day, when we turned off the safe asphalt of the highway onto the dirt road that led to the ranch.

Donna and I loved this leg of any ride home because of the bumps that lifted us off the seat in slow motion. Just before we passed over the dirt viaduct, we always remembered to call out, "Faster, Dad! Make us lose our stomachs," and he rarely refused to indulge us. But this day, there could be no trick driving. It had been an especially wet spring and the rear end of our heavy Pontiac sloughed along in the mud for less than a mile before it slid off the road. My father stepped down hard on the gas, but he was too late.

I loved the excitement of getting stuck in the mud, although I was almost never allowed to witness firsthand the best parts of my father's struggle to free the car. When my mother was with us, she would insist that Donna and I stay inside, so I had to be content with watching the invariable routine from the backseat. My father would begin by swearing under his breath for a minute. Then he would climb out into the mud, turning the wheel over to my mother. Often a good push from him while she spun the wheels would do the trick. This time, it was not enough. Whenever simple manpower didn't work, my father rocked the car back and forth, calling out at the critical moment, "Hit it!" On this day, after several failed rocking maneuvers, the car finally lunged forward up onto the road.

My father kicked the mud off his shoes and got back behind the wheel, smiling broadly, happy with either his skill or his luck, and we made our slow progress on down the road and across the bridge without any more delay. When I climbed out of the car in front of the house, I was still giddy with excitement. I was home.

The next fall, we didn't return to Great Falls. Instead, my mother and father decided to work out a boarding arrangement in Cut Bank, where Donna and I could attend the new parish school. Since there were few enough families willing to take in children during the school year for a few extra dollars, my parents were lucky to find Esther and Hjelmar Slotsvij, a quiet, middle-aged Norwegian carpenter and his energetic, high-spirited wife. They actually liked children but had none of their own. For the next three school years, my sister and I lived with the Slotsvijs during the week in their cosy bungalow, where Esther fussed over us while Hjelmar looked on with indulgent smiles.

The Slotsvijs always seemed genuinely happy to have us around. Esther needed no coaxing at all to pull out her flat grill and make *rullerde pandekager*, airy rolled pancakes that she served not just at breakfast but also as after-school snacks, or with scoops of ice cream for dessert. Always on the watch for the first sign of a cold, she trusted home remedies. Whenever she detected so much as a sniffle, she rushed to concoct a steaming medicinal brew, the fumes of which the patient inhaled from under a towel as he knelt on a chair next to the Wedgewood stove. In his workshop in the basement, Hjelmar made me little wooden trucks and a miniature train and, when I was eight, the best slingshot I've ever owned.

The neighborhood was full of children, and for the first time I had regular playmates besides my sister, particularly Lee Dyrdahl, who lived next door, and the four Newman brothers, two of whom were close to my age and loved to fight. In the fall and spring, we explored the rock formations in the river gorge at the end of the street and played baseball on the vacant lot at the corner. In the winter, we sledded on a nearby street always blocked off after school for this purpose or walked to the ice rink on the southeast side of town to skate. But by the middle of the second grade, marbles had become my sport of choice, and each day at recess, weather permitting, I would rush out into the school yard for a match with my friends.

Even though I developed a passion for marbles and I liked Esther and Hjelmar and my new friends, the best part of this boarding arrangement was that I could go home almost every weekend. On Friday afternoons, as soon as I was released from school, I would race back to the house and kneel on the couch in the front window to watch for my father. I remember being confused that first fall when a car just like ours was sometimes parked down the street and my father did not appear. I liked it best when the first thing I caught sight of as I walked out on Friday afternoons was our cab-over truck waiting in front of the school. "Gotta go," I would call to my friends, as I bolted across the street to the passenger side and climbed up two steps into the familiar warm smell of the cab.

The elementary school that St. Margaret's Parish opened in the fall of 1943 was housed in the old church, which had been left vacant when the new one was built up the hill. The older structure was partitioned into two schoolrooms, each of which accommodated four grades. To maintain order over these mixed assemblages, the two Dominican nuns who made up the entire teaching staff had to be no-nonsense disciplinarians. Sister Joseph, who was in charge of the lower four grades, mobilized pedagogic campaigns and kept a military watch from the back of the room. If a child fidgeted or whispered, she would administer a smart rap to his head with whatever book or folder she happened to be holding, the intensity of the stroke roughly proportional to the magnitude of the infraction.

Each school day began with Mass in the new church, where more often than not Sister Joseph restrained my smiling and whispering, my very breathing, by keeping me next to her in the pew. Close up, she smelled like fresh laundry, a mixed redolence of soap, starch, and ironed cotton. If I so much as smiled over at one of my friends or ventured a word to someone else in the row, she would cut off my peripheral vision for the rest of the service with the sleeve of her habit. Not until third grade, when I had memorized the Latin Mass response card and become an altar boy, did I escape this protective custody.

Like most of my classmates, I usually went to communion because this piety carried with it the privilege of eating one's breakfast during the religion class that followed Mass every morning. Religion and music were the only two disciplines taught to all of us at once. For the rest of the day, Sister drilled lessons with one grade at a time, while the students in the other three worked, or pretended to work, on their assignments.

When Sister Yolanda, who taught music and played the church organ, announced that she would also offer after-school music lessons in the convent across the street, my mother enthusiastically signed both of us up. Donna, she decided, would learn the piano, while I mastered the violin. Under the patient tutelage of this nun, whose own huge hands seemed particularly ill-suited to any instrument, I struggled with my bow for an hour two afternoons a week until I could make my way through a tortured rendition of "Long, Long Ago."

But a chance encounter put an end to my mother's musical ambitions for me. One Friday afternoon, when I was with my father, we passed Whitey McGuire in front of the Smoke House. When he was sober, this big, red-faced Scot, who thought of himself as the tough man of the saloon crowd, usually showed a grudging respect for my father, but on this occasion he had clearly been drinking for several days. Nodding broadly toward the violin case I was carrying, he remarked, "Hey, Bill, I see you're making a real man out of him." My father didn't respond to this aspersion, nor did he bring it up on the ride back to the ranch. But as soon as we arrived home that evening, I took my violin upstairs and put it away in the attic crawl space.

During the summer before my fourth-grade year, the Slotsvijs adopted a child of their own, and my parents had to find us new quarters in town for the next school term. This time we were not as fortunate in our boarding arrangements. When a young couple who had recently moved to Cut Bank advertised for boarders, my mother and father hurried to accept what must have looked like an ideal situation. They themselves had three young children and lived close to the school in a good-sized house, where Donna and I could eat meals with the family and do our lessons and sleep in two nicely finished basement rooms.

I disliked almost everything about living with this family. They were not bad people, I suppose, but in this household my sister and I always felt like outsiders, intruders almost. And, since our rooms in the basement turned out to be virtually unheated, they offered no refuge away from the inhospitable family quarters. The wife presided at meals, carefully controlling the size of the portions and reserving any food she considered a treat for her children alone. I remember her keeping an especially close guard on a jar of mint jelly, whisking it away if she imagined that Donna or I meant to sample it. I didn't care much for mint jelly—at home it appeared on the table in a cut-glass bowl whenever we had lamb—but I resented this exclusion nonetheless. Worst of all were those times when her father, who had suffered a stroke, ate at the table. Paralyzed on one side and with a right eye that exuded a thick, yellowish ooze, he always sat opposite me. On these occasions, I often excused myself before I had finished my food.

But I was old enough by this time to escape from the household in the hours after school by playing outside with my friends. Once it was too cold for marbles, we trudged from the school yard to a hill near the Slotsvijs' house, where the city closed off traffic on two long blocks every afternoon until five. Here, with kids from all over the north side of town, we waxed the metal runners of our Flexible Flyers for exhilarating runs down the icy slope. Since terrifying speeds could be achieved with the weight of a double-layered sled, the older boys liked to cadge rides on top of the sleds of children too young to do more than whimper.

On an afternoon late that winter when most of the sledders had already dragged themselves home—it must have been after five because the traffic barrier had been taken down—one of these older boys decided to make a final run by himself. He was hit by a car in the intersection at the bottom of the hill. We crowded around as the driver and another man carried the boy into the Slotsvijs' living room to wait for Dr. Olsen. I could see that he had been badly hurt, but still he was conscious and looking around at us. The next day at school, when someone told me that he had died, I didn't believe it.

Long Winters

Through all the milder seasons of the year, sheep act the pattern of domestication. Depending as much on the herder's hand as on their own brute sense to keep out of harm's way, they still are peevish at most human meddling. And, more than that, they can be the jitteriest creatures—high strung and excitable; once spooked, impossible to control. So they wander and graze over summer pastures, willy nilly, looking for all the world indifferent to what's good for them.

But sheep are wiser in the ways of nature than those who've never lived through a winter with them might imagine. When the snow begins to fall, they show what they are made of. Given half a chance by the weather, they'll forage stubbornly across the frozen ranges, pawing the snow all day to uncover the curly brown grass underneath, lifting out the pickings with their noses. At night, they huddle in small bands against the arctic cold, and if a blizzard traps them in an icy drift, they'll paw toward safety for as long as they have breath. Still, even when they soldiered up in the battle for their own survival, our sheep left us plenty to worry about during the long Montana winters.

From November until April, we redrew the borders of the ranch and kept our bands closer to home. To lend them a little shelter from the worst of the night winds, we set up circles of panels and protected the north sides of these with stacked bales of straw. When the snow pack was too deep or the ground too frozen for them to forage on their narrowed ranges, the herders kept the sheep in their corrals all day except for those times when we hitched up horses to the sled and fed them Dakota hay and oil cake off the back. Even on the level terrain close to the ranch, the long-haired winter team would start the pull slowly, leaning into the harnesses to keep their footing on the frozen ground. Their warm breath fogged the air, first on one side, then the other, as they plodded along in front of the loaded sled.

After my father bought the cab-over truck in 1946, we used the horses less. I liked to dribble oil cake from a burlap sack and watch the sheep nibble their way along behind us in the rutted double trail the wheels made in the snow. A few eager members of each band would rush ahead each time a burst of pellets scattered on the ground. Sometimes, if I was lucky and Jimmy was busy at some other job, my father would commission me to kneel on the seat of the cab and steer the truck, with its manual throttle set at slow, while he and the herder cut the wires from the bales of hay and pitched it off the back. I quickly discovered that if I slipped down off the seat and stood beside the wheel, I could gain enough leverage to operate the gas pedal as well. But, invariably, my foot would slip and give me away with a lurch at the rear of the truck, and I would be sternly instructed to stick to steering.

At times winter kept both the sheep and the herders snug in their corrals and wagons. In the worst of blizzards, the herder tied a rope from the wheel of his wagon to the corral gate so he could find his way to the band. Dad always reminded Jimmy to make the corrals large enough to allow the sheep room to mill about and avoid stacking. When the temperature dipped below zero for several days, my father would bring coal instead of wood to warm the wagons all night without repeated stokings.

Not all the herders lasted through the long months of cold and hazardous storms, but Andy thrived on them. He wore the same layered clothing year-round, and his gasoline generator gave him electricity for a portable heater, a percolator coffeepot, and a Zenith Transatlantic radio. He found reading on the full-size bed—

and a day off—preferable to tracking a fast-grazing band during the first green grass of spring.

Herders looked different in the winter, with a dusting of frost on their eyebrows, the hair in their noses, and their whiskers. Figured against the snow and patches of brown earth, they were easy to spot as our truck ground toward the camps loaded with hay. They walked steadily all day, circling their bands, slapping their shoulders now and then to keep the blood flowing to the tips of their fingers. Andy avoided the frost on his mustache by wearing a heavy wool scarf wrapped around the lower half of his face. His hands were never cold in the army surplus mittens he wore; they had wool inserts he changed off and on during the day to keep his hands dry. Wet meant cold, as Andy knew well from his time on the north range.

In 1945 the first winter storm arrived early, while our sheep were still scattered. Although the herders struggled through a blizzard that continued for days and managed to corral most of our flock, two bands were left stranded near the coulee by the reservoir. My father headed out alone to find them but was stopped at the gate to the north range by waist-high drifts that even the jeep couldn't plow through. Unless another way could be found to reach the stranded sheep and lead them back to shelter, they would be buried and freeze to death. Wasting no time, my father drove over the clearer back roads to the oil fields north of Cut Bank. There, he convinced the owner of a bulldozer that it would be worth his time to dig out the sheep and clear a path for them across the snowpack.

The next morning, the snow had stopped falling and the wind had died down. The glare of the sun on the snow was so bright I had to squint as I watched my father and the bulldozer owner set off to find the stranded sheep. I was disappointed that there was no room in the cab for me to go along, but I heard the whole account of this adventure when they returned late that afternoon with a thousand sheep from one of the bands struggling along on their short legs in the graded path plowed for them by the bulldozer.

At the reservoir, my father had judged the positions of the huddles, buried by this time in deep drifts, and directed the other man while he cleared narrow swaths with the bulldozer's huge blade. By midafternoon, the two of them had managed to free all but two hundred of the trapped sheep from their icy imprisonment. The second band, which had been scattered in smaller groups across a wider area, hadn't fared so well, but we didn't know the extent of our losses until several weeks later when a chinook thawed most of the deep snowpack. Nearly a third of this band had suffocated or been frozen in the drifts.

Despite the somber mood caused by this loss, the daily trips I made with my father to check on the surviving sheep were more exhilarating than any experience I had ever had. On clear days, we bumped across a terrain of almost blinding brightness. Near sunset, rainbow-colored sundogs—"mock suns" on a solar halo—kept a hovering watch near the horizon. Heavy with oil cake sacks roped to the front fenders, the jeep clanged along on chained wheels, and its engine made a sudden labored hum each time it powered us through a lingering drift, sending pikes of snow across the hood. The wipers struggled to keep up with the flying snow, while the little fan churned away to defog the windows on the driver's side. Holding on to the passenger's grip handle and leaning forward, I would reach up to wipe the glass on my side with the palm of my mitten, blinking at each splay of tiny frozen crystals across the windshield. Not quite knowing where we were going or what would happen next fueled my high excitement.

1945 had been an anxious time for my parents for other reasons, too. Even after Japan's surrender, no news arrived for weeks about my Uncle Dubs, who had been a prisoner of war in Okinawa for more than three years. Finally, late in September, my uncle called us from Letterman Army Hospital in San Francisco; he was alive and, if not well, at least recovering from his ordeal. Dubs was a tall man, well over six feet, but when he was released from the Japanese camp, he weighed only 98 pounds and was seriously ill with malaria and beriberi. By mid-December, he was well enough to make the trip back to Cut Bank on the train.

I remember that first holiday after the war as the Christmas of the trains. Three different wind-up sets materialized under the tree, the separate gifts to me from my parents, Dubs, and his good friend, Chuck Cooper, who was also back from the war and staying the winter with us. The adults enjoyed this chance superfluity as much as I did; long after I had been sent off to bed, I could hear the three men crashing the wind-up toys into each other in the living room. Although my uncle was still terribly thin and suffering from recurrent fevers, he hadn't lost his easy manner or his sense of humor. When my father donated cases of sauerkraut to the church food drive for German refugees, Dubs and Chuck laughed about the joke for days.

Every year right after Christmas, we left the sheep in Jimmy's and the herders' care and went into town to stay with the Nadeaus. This holiday from the winter worries and isolation always lasted from the day after Christmas until New Year's. For a full week, my father and Wilfred would celebrate their friendship. And, nothing—not the weather, not work, not wives or children—ever interfered with their annual bonding.

The Nadeaus lived in the finest house in Cut Bank, an Art Deco affair with five bedrooms and four baths, palatial by our reservation ranchhouse standards. Just inside the front door off the foyer, Wilfred kept an office, furnished lawyerlike with a leather couch

My parents brave the winter storm of 1947

and a huge partners' desk. On the opposite side of the entryway, a wall of curved glass tiles faced the street in the living room, which was illuminated by fluorescent lights built into the ceiling moldings. The kitchen was equipped with the latest appliances, even a dishwasher, and featured a red vinyl booth built into the wall under a bank of plate glass windows. The table in the dining room seated twelve.

During these holidays, while the women shopped or visited with friends and the kids played at the house, Wilfred and my father did a little business in the mornings and wound out the afternoons drinking at the Elks Club. When the men returned home each evening, our two families would eat dinner together in the dining room. Even the children dressed up for these many-course meals, which featured special food the men had ordered and shipped in—fresh Pacific salmon or Alaskan crab, lobsters we ate with tiny forks.

These days in town always gave me a fresh view of my parents. At home, my father wore laced cowboy boots and heavy canvas trousers and flannel shirts, but during our annual holiday, he appeared every morning in a white shirt and gabardine slacks, a leather jacket and city shoes. My mother exchanged her wraparound cotton housedresses and aprons for smart wool suits. Although we always wore our good clothes when we went to church, my father pulled off his tie even before we piled back into the car after Mass. For this single week of the year, the adults stayed dressed up all day.

After dinner, the adults might return to the Elks Club, bringing other ranchers and local businessmen and their wives back to the house to extend a party that was still going strong when the place closed. This group almost always included a shapely blonde who was the local hairdresser and her much shorter husband, who wore a thin Clark Gable mustache and flashy pin-striped suits. The soirees went on late into the night, their music and hilarity and loud discourse audible to us in the bedrooms below. Before the week was out, my mother would have had enough of noisy celebration and suggest to my father that it was time to return to the ranch. His response—or Wilfred's, if he'd heard her plea—was a standard joke: "Time to call the little lady a cab," one or the other would call out.

If they grew tired of the local scene, my father and Wilfred would find new stomping grounds. Leaving wives and children behind, they might drive or even fly off to another town to do some business or to see a friend. One year, when they had driven up to Hungry Horse, where Wilfred owned a drug store, they found themselves at the end of the day in a saloon in Kalispell. The place was called the Swan Bar, either for the nearby mountain range or the dovelike creature painted on the sign that hung out front. When Wilfred couldn't get the piano player there to hammer out a song he wanted to hear, he offered to buy the bar so he could fire him. More than happy to have someone take the place off his hands, the owner struck a deal with Wilfred, and in the mood of the moment, my father agreed to enter the saloon business as his partner.

I enjoyed our week at the Nadeaus nearly as much as Dad. After the flamboyant style of his father, Gary Nadeau played with toys as big as life. Outside behind the garage, he had a ten-foot oil derrick with a bit to pound holes in the ground. His midget car—a replica of a Bugatti racer more elegant than the Doodle Bug I had yearned for—was equipped with a single-cylinder engine, connected by belts to its motorcycle transmission, and a miniature clutch and brake pedal. And in the basement Gary kept a model train that was almost too much for two boys to operate. A few feet above the floor in a space larger than most living rooms, three engines smoked and sounded whistles and flashed lights as they pulled coal and box and flatbed cars through tunnels and over bridges on a landscape of forests and mountains, farms and villages and stations.

But my most vivid memories of Gary's basement playroom center not on the train but rather on the boxing equipment Wilfred and my father set up there for us: a heavy punching bag filled with sawdust, a smaller pear-shaped bag lowered to the reach of shorter boys, wooden-handled skipping ropes, and calisthenics mats. This training gym was my father's idea, part of his plan for me. He wanted me to learn how to handle myself and believed that I should be brought along early in the skills he had found useful in his own life. Wilfred went in with him on the gear and provided the room, where, not just at Christmas but also every Tuesday and Thursday afternoon for two school terms, Joe Henderson was hired to teach Gary and me to box. Joe was a stocky, middle-aged black man who had boxed as a Chicago club fighter in his youth. Now he worked as a porter for the Great Northern and used the extra money he made shining shoes at a local barbershop during his layovers to finance his avocation as the town bookie.

Gary hated these sessions, especially the sparring exercises, so Joe started bringing other kids along as sparring partners. In the beginning, I was also a reluctant participant. I would have preferred to be playing marbles or basketball. The training sessions were demanding, since Joe insisted on push-ups, sit-ups, rope jumping, bag work, and sparring at every workout. After a while, though, I began to take to the sport, perhaps because I had always listened to the Friday night fights with my father, perhaps because I discovered that with the skills Joe taught me and my naturally fast hands, few boys my age could stay with me in the sparring sessions. Whatever the case, Joe was a good teacher, and years later I still boxed well enough to be assigned the gym teachers rather than other students as my opponents in school bouts.

It was also Joe who first introduced me to the previously unthinkable possibility that my father wasn't the strongest man in the world. If Dad happened to be in Cut Bank on an afternoon when we were training, he would stop in to watch, and occasionally to box with Joe himself. Over the years, I had watched my father handle difficult men at the ranch and more than once seen him return from the Smoke House with a puffed lip and the satisfied look he got after he'd had more than words with some quarrelsome local. But the first time he and Joe sparred, I was stunned to see him wince in pain under a rain of solid body blows. My father was the bigger man and had the faster hands, but Joe's skills in the ring made him the better fighter.

The Last Season

In the day of his work

when the grace of the world

was upon him, he made his way,

not turning back or looking aside,

light in his stride.

Now may the grace of death

be upon him, his spirit blessed

in deep song of the world

and the stars turning, the seasons

returning, and long rest.

—WENDELL BERRY

Summer of 1948

When I arrived home for summer vacation late in May of 1948, my father presented me with a new pump-action .22 rifle and taught me to use it. In the lingering daylight after supper every evening, Dad and I set tin cans on the garden fence posts facing the hill and practiced shooting them off. Unlike my BB gun, this adult weapon was a lot of trouble. I had to worry about the safety catch and pay attention to where the gun was pointed; the stock had to be sleeved in a canvas cover when I wasn't using it so it wouldn't get scratched. Still, I enjoyed these companionable target practice sessions, and by July I had become a good enough shot to be a real threat to the residents of the gopher town on the hill above the storage area.

Soon it became clear that the rifle was not just an exciting new toy but part of a larger plan my father had to make me more self-sufficient and independent. Now that I was ten, he announced, I was old enough to become more than an errand boy. From now on, I would assume the role of an employee—a full member of the crew—and be paid two dollars a day for my services. I was elated with the prospect of this elevated status, more excited than I had been about the rifle by half, and could hardly wait to begin my new job. Most of the boys I knew were still playing around the house while their fathers went somewhere else to work. This, I was sure, was going to be the best summer of my life.

As it turned out, my career as a paid ranch hand was short-lived. My first assignment was to help two of the men repack sacks of wool that had been soaked in an early summer downpour. I was throwing dried fleeces from the base of the free-standing platform we had set up for the job when a sudden gust of wind toppled the structure and an angle brace fell on my right knee. My leg wasn't broken, but it was too swollen to walk on for several days. Late that afternoon, when my father returned from Great Falls and found me propped up with an ice pack on the porch daybed, he scowled as he knelt to inspect my knee. He gave me two silver dollars for that day's work but no more was said about my formal employment.

Even though this accident cut short my days as a paid member of the crew, my father continued to bring me along in new jobs and delegate more responsibility to me in the next few months. During shearing, I learned to tie fleeces well enough that the bundles survived the hoist up onto the platform without coming undone. When I wasn't tieing and throwing, I helped to administer first aid to sheep that had been nicked by the clippers and to weigh and mark packed wool sacks. As always, I went along when the sheep were trailed to the mountains, this time on horseback. At haying time, I worked with my father to repair sickle blades and mend hay nets, and when Charlie Cree Medicine and his crew arrived to put up the alfalfa, I ran the rake during the men's breaks and was sometimes even sent out by myself in the jeep to deliver water or a new blade to them in the fields.

Through the summer, I came to feel more and more like my father's full partner as well as his sidekick. Shadowing his movements through each work day, I acted as his memory, reminding him of what he had forgotten as he gathered materials for the next task. Most gratifying of all, he trusted me to drive more often while he relaxed and sometimes even napped on our trips to tend camp. Without comment, Dad would simply climb into the truck on the passenger side when it was time to start out for the north range, and I would rush to take the wheel.

I could not imagine life away from the ranch, but for the first time my father began to talk about leaving. Tired of split half partnerships and reservation land leases, nervous about the decline in the wool and lamb markets, he spoke of getting his own place, a cattle ranch this time, or becoming a livestock buyer for one of the big meat processors. At noon, he turned up the volume and leaned toward the radio to catch the daily livestock report quotes. My mother was less sanguine about leaving the ranch and the uncertainty that such a change would bring. I was content with things just the way they were.

It was so dry that summer that even in the meadows above Heart Butte the pasturage was barely adequate, and the sheep had to be moved along every few days to new ranges. Several days before we were to leave for our annual week at Swan Lake, my father made a final overnight run to the mountains. I don't remember the reason now, but for the first time all summer, I didn't tag along.

On and off for several months, Dad had complained about a pain in his stomach, serious enough that he had even consulted Dr. Olsen, who advised him to drink milk or eat a saltine cracker to ease the discomfort. When he returned from the mountains that Sunday night early in August, he was feeling so ill from one of these attacks that he went right to bed. But the next morning at breakfast, he announced that a good night's sleep had cured his problem and he set out for town to run an errand or two and get supplies. I was busy getting my fishing poles and shooting gear in order for our vacation. For the second time in as many days, I stayed home.

After lunch that day, I went down to the river to try out a new reel. I was just returning when Wilfred pulled up in the yard and rushed into the house to find my mother. A few minutes later, she hurried down the steps with him, wiping her hands on her apron, and herded the three of us into the backseat of Wilfred's car. On the way into town, he told us what had happened. My father had met him for lunch at the cafe down the street from his office, but before they had even started to eat, Dad had doubled over in pain. Wilfred had taken him out to the hospital, where the cause of his stomach cramps had been diagnosed as an inflamed, perhaps already burst, appendix. He had been rushed into surgery.

By the time Wilfred drove us into Cut Bank, Dad's appendix had been removed and he had been taken into the recovery room. Mother left my two sisters and me in the hospital lounge while she and Wilfred went off to find the doctor. In this area adjoining the main lobby, Donna and I sat silently next to each other on a couch watching people come and go at the reception desk near the front door while Joleen played with her doll on the floor. I thought about my father lying somewhere beyond the double doors at the end of the hall, but I couldn't imagine what he would look like in a hospital bed. Already I began to regret that I hadn't gone along with him to Heart Butte. If I had been there, I wondered, would I have seen that he was more than a little sick and convinced him to go right to the doctor instead of driving back home?

We probably didn't have to wait more than twenty minutes, although it seemed a longer time. Joleen had grown tired of wrapping and unwrapping her doll in its blanket and had started running back and forth between the reception desk and the front door. I had just got up from the couch to bring her back into the lounge when Mother and Wilfred reappeared at the end of the hall with Dr. Olsen. The three of them stood there talking for a moment in front of the double doors. Wilfred had his arm around Mother's shoulders. She had been crying, I could see. When I ran up to them to ask about Dad, the three adults stopped talking. Instead of answering my questions, Wilfred took Joleen by the hand and nodded for Donna and me to come along with him. At the front door, I turned back to see my mother slump down onto the couch we had been sitting on. Dr. Olsen was leaning over her, patting her shoulder and talking quietly.

For the next four days, my sisters and I stayed at the Nadeaus' house while the adults went back and forth to the hospital. Since my father was not allowed visitors, a stream of friends came and went at the house to express their concern and ask about his condition. On Monday and Tuesday when Mother and Wilfred returned from the hospital, their responses to Donna's and my questions were evasive. We could go see Dad "as soon as he was a little better," they told us. On Wednesday, Wilfred took me aside and said that he would take us to see my father the next day, but on Thursday he put me off again. "Maybe tomorrow," was all he said when I pressed him. Finally, on Friday morning, my sisters and I were told we could come along when the adults set out for the hospital.

When I was four, I had spent two days in the Cut Bank Hospital with a lingering middle ear infection that had ripened into mastoiditis. As my sisters and I followed Mother through the double doors off the lobby and trailed along down the hall behind her and one of the nurses, the smell of disinfectant and the sound of a metal-wheeled trolley rattling over the linoleum floor awakened my memory of that feverish interlude. A little more than halfway down the hall, Mother stopped in front of the open door of one of the rooms and the three of us crowded into the doorway around her.

Dad lay on a partially elevated bed in the center of the room. He was breathing heavily—there were oxygen tubes in his nose—and his eyes were closed. Another tube snaked its way from a needle in his arm to a bottle of clear liquid hanging from a pole next to the bed. I know now that he was in a coma, but to my eyes then he was simply sleeping. I looked up at Mother, waiting for her to usher us into the room, to wake Dad up so that he could see that we had finally been brought to visit him, but even when I pulled at her hand, she didn't move or speak. After the four of us had stood in a silent, rigid line on the threshold for several moments, someone, the nurse probably, cupped her hands around my shoulders and gently moved me away from the doorway. "I guess we should leave now," Mother said.

This was the last time I saw my father alive. Two and a half hours later, at a few minutes after 1 P.M. on August 6, 1948, he died, eighty-eight days after his thirty-seventh birthday. I was three months short of eleven; Donna was almost twelve, and Joleen had just turned five. My mother was a widow at thirty-five.

In the intervening years, I have often reconstructed that Friday afternoon. Donna and I were outside in the front yard with Gary when Mother returned from the hospital. She called the two of us into the living room and told us that Dad had just died. Although I'm sure that I didn't understand the meaning of what she was saying, I erupted in convulsive sobs. As my wails eventually subsided into erratic hiccups, Mother silently placed her rosary in my hand, and for a few moments I tried to mouth the words of familiar prayers, but they neither comforted nor distracted me. I wanted to be hugged and talked to. I wanted someone to tell me exactly what had happened. How could a strong person like my father be dead? Death was something that happened to people who were old or weak or not paying attention. I closed and opened my eyes hard again and again to clear my blurred vision, but each time they refilled with tears. I laid the rosary down.

What naive impulse still makes me wonder that none of the experiences of my first ten years helped me in the smallest way to understand my father's death? I had witnessed the mystery of life's beginnings and endings hundreds of times. I had watched the struggles of birthing ewes and their drops, observed swallows while they waited for their chicks to hatch. I had seen my father chop the head off a young rooster, had studied his deliberate motions when he butchered a yearling. I myself had taken part in the rites of nature, stepped forward to intervene in its cycles, shooting swallows, killing gophers and coyotes, flushing rabbits from their nests in the alfalfa to save them from the destruction of the mower's whirring blades. But no thought about the mortal affinity of all the creatures on nature's great chain of being had ever crossed my mind, and if it had, it could not have made this central cataclysm of my life more comprehensible to me.

Even now when I think about my father, what I remember first, most, is the sudden loss of him, while I acquiesce to my own dying, a little at a time. It is as if all my memories of our time together have been folded into an amalgam of sadness. I am still swamped by the waves of sorrow I felt when he died. Even now, I revisit the bright happiness of my childhood, recall the pleasures of the long days I spent at my father's side—watching him, learning lessons he meant to teach me—only after I have struggled once again through the dark currents of that early grief.

Wilfred leads me by the hand across a room in the funeral parlor to a coffin on a dais. Inside this glossy, bronze-colored box, my father lies with his head resting on a narrow pillow made of the same silky fabric that tufts the interior sides and opened lid. His face is smoky white, as if it has been daubed with powder. His hands are folded across the vest of the unfamiliar brown suit he is wearing. I reach into the box and touch his chest, before always warm and pliant when I've leaned against it; it is hard now, and cold. My throat constricts when I try to swallow. Wilfred puts his hands on my shoulders to move me away, but I pull back long enough to reach over again, raise one inert hand and push the rosary Mother has given me under it.

I sit between my mother and my older sister in the first pew at St. Margaret's Church. On the other side of the aisle are the six pall-bearers, my father's good friends, Wilfred Nadeau and Conrad Bradley, Johnny Sullivan and Orville Thomas; his business partner, Art Pardue, and Art's son, Kenny. In the aisle between us on a metal rack is the casket, closed now and draped in a white cloth with a crucifix on top. Behind us sit the members of my mother's family, Dad's brother and sister and their families, other friends. Scattered in the back pews of the church are herders and ranch hands, some of whom I haven't seen for a year or two. Jimmy, my father's foreman, looks like someone else in his ill-fitting blue suit.

While Father Hieptas drones the Latin words of the funeral Mass, I stare at the cloth-draped box. Even though I have seen my father there, I can't evoke the image of him lying inside it. The priest moves down from the altar and circles the casket, swinging the heavy censor over it, around it, as he goes. Along with the familiar pungency of the incense, another odor, a sour suffusion that I don't recognize, permeates the church. I have never smelled cut florist's flowers before and it will be years later, at another funeral, before I connect the baskets of carnations banking the altar with this almost sickening stench.

In dreamlike slow motion, we pass through the doors of the church and down the front steps—the people milling there move back to open a path for the four of us—to a black limousine parked at the curb. Francis Sullivan, Johnny's youngest son, who owns a funeral home in Great Falls, helps my mother and the two girls into the backseat and then I climb in and sit facing them on one of the fold-down jump seats. The car door stands open while a dozen of my mother's and father's friends lean in, one at a time, to pat my mother's hand, to kiss or hug one or another of us. These people, all of whom I know well, seem suddenly tentative, shy almost, and move away after a nervous word or two as though they are trying to get out of the way of those behind them. Finally, someone outside shuts the door and the limousine pulls away from the curb.

Behind the hearse, the limousine slowly leads the line of cars east through town and turns north onto the Santa Rita Road, the same back road we have always taken on icy winter days and whenever the river is swollen in late spring. As we move past the familiar oil field equipment strung along the side of the road, a single sentence from Father Hieptas's short homily echoes in my mind: "Losing such a young husband, father, and friend is a sorrow to all of us, but we must see it as part of God's plan." I flounder in the senseless words of the platitude. My father's death could not have been a part of any plan.

At the cemetery, the limousine turns right onto the first gravel lane and stops. The door opens and Francis helps my mother out. My sisters and I follow her up onto the lawn to a carpet of imitation grass where the pallbearers are struggling to set the casket down on two woven straps tightly stretched across a rectangular chrome frame. Mother sits down in one of the white folding chairs that have been set up in two rows on one side of the casket and holds Joleen in front of her. Only after I have taken the seat next to them do I notice the dark gap at the edge of the casket and understand that there is a hole underneath it.

As other mourners come up onto the lawn to take seats behind us and stand around the grave, the priest arranges the white cloth on the casket, lays the wire mesh crucifix on top of it. He begins to chant prayers, first in Latin, then in English. On the opposite side of the grave, Wilfred and Conrad stand stony-faced and rigid. Conrad's lower lip is tucked under his front teeth and tears streak his round cheeks. I have never seen a man cry before. My uncle Dubs stares at the ground and holds the hand of Mary, his young wife. He looks more angry than sad. Behind us, I can hear the sobs of my father's sister, Esther, above the words the priest is chanting as he circles the grave and sprinkles holy water on the casket.

The priest finishes his prayers and the mourners move away from the grave and trail back toward their cars. As I numbly follow my mother and sisters across the lawn, I try to shake myself out of the torpor that has settled over me. I want to refocus my attention on Dad, to make some sense of this place. But I am light-headed, almost dizzy, and I can't concentrate. I feel almost transparent. The casket is still lying on the chrome frame when we drive out of the cemetery and turn onto the highway. How long will it be left there, I wonder. I do not yet try to imagine the casket being lowered into the black hole and shoveled over with dirt.

Although there are cars parked everywhere around the yard when we arrive home, the ranch seems unnaturally still. Inside, dozens of people move from room to room, talking and eating the food friends and neighbors have laid out on the dining room table. Everywhere I go, I am greeted with easy pats and hugs and kind words, which I try to acknowledge politely. Someone hands me a plate of chicken and Jell-O and potato salad. I poke at it, unable to eat, and try to answer hollow, solicitous questions, confusingly upbeat, about school and sports. Finally, I escape to my room and change my clothes. Leaving by the back door, I start out toward the river. Rebba Nadeau calls after me hesitantly, "Wait for me." She catches up and the two of us walk along silently past the weatherbreak behind the house. Even the leaves of the cottonwoods there are motionless.

Afterward

In years, and in the numbering of space,

Moving away from what we grew to know,

We stray like paper blown from place to place,

Impelled by every element to go.

(I think of haying on an August day,

Forking the stacks of hay.)

We can remember trees and attitudes

That foreign landscapes do not imitate;

They grow distinct within the interludes

Of memory beneath a stranger state.

—DONALD HALL

The First Year

Of course, we did not take a vacation that August. Never again did my family go up to Glacier Park for the day or make the trip over to Swan Lake. Instead, in the weeks after my father's funeral, we all simply tried to cope with the day-to-day routines of ranch life without him. Mother struggled to make sense of the agreements Dad had made with his partner, Art Pardue—many of these had been oral—and worked her way through insurance policies and loans and bank accounts. Several times each week, she went into town to talk to John Green, her attorney, about settling the estate. Ida took care of Joleen and the cooking and the housework, while Jimmy and the herders handled the sheep and everything else that had to be done outside.

During the last weeks of August, I became consumed with the particulars of ranch management and worried almost obsessively that things were not being done as Dad would have wanted. I shadowed Jimmy's steps, going along with him to tend camp, to meet the hay trucks from South Dakota and haul oil cake in from the railroad boxcars at Fort Piegan. I interrupted him a dozen times a day to question some decision, reminded him over and over to check all the details. Although he might well have taken offense at this proprietary attitude, he was kind enough to keep the peace and let my nervous interference pass without remark. And he probably took comfort in a fact that had slipped my mind altogether: It was almost September and I would be leaving the ranch before long. But I was so absorbed in my self-imposed role of overseer that it came as a shock when my mother announced one morning near the end of the month that Donna and I would be spending that school year in Great Falls.

In the fall of 1948, my sister and I were once again separated, this time by more than a few rooms. I stayed with my father's brother, Dubs, and his wife, Mary, while Donna lived on the other side of Great Falls with the Sullivans, my parents' long-time friends. My uncle was a less exuberant personality than my father, quieter and more tentative, but like Dad he loved dogs and horses, hunting and stream fishing, and he had an easy way with children that made me like him a lot. He had been only twenty-eight years old when he came home from the war. Three years later, he was still spending months at a time in a Tacoma veterans' hospital, where military doctors removed the shrapnel from his body and treated the lingering effects of malaria, fused his bayonetted right arm, and inserted a steel plate in the place of a shattered hipbone.

In the long stretches when Dubs was away from home, Mary did everything she could to comfort me and make up for his absence. Only twenty-one herself, with a full-time job and a baby of her own, she found time to fuss over me, to worry about my well-being and state of mind. She kept up a steady stream of cheerful discourse, more monologue than conversation, as she unloaded groceries and cooked our dinner, washed the dishes, and bathed the baby. She would draw me out of the worst of my dolor and homesickness with stories about her day and friendly inquiries about mine. When she noticed that there were no other children my age in the neighborhood, she bought me a bicycle; now I could travel farther afield to play with the new friends she was sure I would make at school, she announced. As ready as she must have been by Sunday to put her feet up and relax, more often than not she would bundle up the baby and the three of us would travel across town on the bus to see Donna at the Sullivans'.

At Christmas, when heavy snows stranded us in Great Falls, Mary engaged me in decorating an elaborate tree and cooked a big holiday dinner for just the two of us. Still, even with this solicitous attention, most afternoons that fall and winter while I waited for her to return from work, I simply pedaled aimlessly up and down the block, alone and confused and sorry for myself.

In bed at night, my melancholia materialized in frightening spatial disorientations, which bothered me nearly as much as the psychological dispossession that caused them. After Mary had kissed me good-night and closed my door, the tiny room I slept in would expand around me, while my body seemed to pull away from its anchoring surroundings. To overcome these feelings of disjunction, I mentally traced the outline of my limbs under the sheets and blankets. Finally, I would blot out the alarming perception that I had been disconnected, cut loose from all of the material world, by curling myself into a tight ball. By the time I nodded off with my hands jammed under my head, the pillow would be damp from my tears.

During the day, I wrestled with more matter-of-fact problems of adjustment. Each morning Mary handed me a neatly packed lunch and waited with me for the city bus to pull up at the corner. The warm leather smell that met me as I boarded always reminded me of the Sunday outings Donna and I had taken with Aunt Cora during our earlier exile in Great Falls. Two miles down the line, I disembarked at Our Lady of Lourdes School. Here, for the first time, I was in a single-grade classroom, but I didn't take much interest in any of the advantages this situation offered. Outside on the playground, I got into one bloody-nosed scuffle after another, picking fights with other boys on the slightest provocation, sometimes for no reason at all. At least once a week I would be collared by the nun on recess duty and sent off to be talked to by the principal. He was a soft-spoken, easy-going man, who wearily rubbed the bridge of his nose as he admonished me for not controlling what he referred to cryptically as "my temper."

Certainly there must have been any number of hours during these days at school when I was not burdened by either moroseness or hostility, but I remember only a single incident of pure, hilarious release. It happened in the fifth-grade classroom just before the December vacation, when Sister Agnes was reading us the familiar story of Joseph's and Mary's desperate search for a place to rest on the first Christmas Eve. "Turned away from first one inn and then another," she solemnly intoned, "Joseph helped Mary climb back on her ass." The bawdy ambiguity I snagged from the final phrase sent me into an uncontrollable fit of giggling. Still choking with laughter, I was led upstairs again to the principal's office. This time, he didn't mention my temper but lectured me more sternly than usual on my lack of respect for "our Savior."

Early in the spring, Dubs was pronounced well enough to be released from the hospital in Tacoma, and, still limping on his repaired hip and with his right arm in a sling, he returned to his family for good. Either by nature or because of the pins and plates that had been used to cobble his broken body together, he moved more slowly than my father and he was certainly less volatile, but like Dad he had inherited their German mother's rage for order. During the three months of recuperative leave he had been granted before he was to report for his new job at the Air Force base in Great Falls, I helped him set up a workshop and make repairs and improvements to the little house we were living in. Together, we reroofed the leaky garage and built bathroom cabinets and planted a small garden out back. After school and on Saturdays, as we sawed and hammered together in companionable silence, my black moods would lift, and for hours at a time I would forget to be sad or hostile or homesick.

Whenever Sunday was warm and clear, Dubs took me fishing. As a rule, Mary would pack a picnic and come along with Baby

Wayne to watch while we tried our luck with his collection of flies for a few afternoon hours on a stream close to home. But a couple of times, my uncle and I set out earlier in the day by ourselves and made the two-hour trip to Little Badger Creek near Dupuyer, where he and my father had fished as boys. As his old Plymouth rattled along over washboard roads through the landscape of their childhood, Dubs grew uncharacteristically voluble, spinning out stories about their youthful fishing and hunting escapades. Some of these tales I had never heard before, and I suspect my uncle exaggerated any number of details for dramatic effect. In the one I liked best, my father—in his brother's memory and in my imagination, as big and strong as a latter-day Paul Bunyan—grabbed the antlers of a wounded elk that had knocked him to the ground with a scissors kick and hung on as the stunned animal clambered to its feet and careened around the clearing. In the end, Dubs himself had been the one to put the elk out of its misery and release its dizzy passenger onto the ground by having the presence of mind to shoot the poor animal a second time.

While I struggled through these months to regain my equilibrium, my sister battled whatever demons she had to cope with on the other side of town. In accordance with the conspiracy of silence members of my family have always taken part in, Donna and I didn't try to console each other then, and in the years since, I've never managed to pry from her the particulars of her own Great Falls banishment. At home my mother was wrestling with the problems of running the ranch by herself. Jimmy Dunbar had convinced her that, with his help, she could see the lambs my father had bought the previous spring through the year. Dakota hay and oil cake had already been paid for and delivered. After the sheep had been wintered, Jimmy reasoned, he and my mother could oversee shearing late in the spring, move the flocks to the mountains at midsummer, and bring them back in time for a fall sale. During these months, while she thought about whether to keep the ranch or sell out, Art Pardue could look around for a new partner, and in the meantime he would be willing to handle the lease renewals and bank business in Great Falls.

Mother really didn't have much choice but to follow Jimmy's coaxing. She and my father had arrived at the ranch with precious little, and in the half dozen years since, they had planned carefully and worked hard and had watched—cautiously hopeful at first, later in less restrained delight at their luck—as their paltry stake doubled and redoubled during the war. For the first time in her life, my mother had felt that, although they were hardly rich, they had managed to attain what her own mother would have called "gracious plenty." She couldn't bring herself to swallow the losses an abrupt sellout would have brought with it. Besides, even though the war was over, wool and meat prices were holding firm, and she had Jimmy's assurances that the two of them would be able to carry on together. She squared her shoulders and pushed through the winter.

But by early spring the burden my mother had taken on had worn her thin. She passed up the option for a fall delivery of lambs and, still unresolved about what should happen next, looked forward to the prospect of selling the yearlings. The decisive moment came on the day her car was almost hit by a Great Northern freight train two miles from the ranch. On her way into town, she had been so preoccupied with worry about an outbreak of pinkeye in one of the bands that she didn't hear the warning blast and drove across the tracks an instant before the freight reached the crossing. While the train clattered along behind her, she pulled her car over onto the shoulder of the road and turned off its engine. By the time she had stopped shaking, she had made up her mind to sell her share of the sheep, the leases, and the equipment and move to town in the fall.

When the school year ended in late May and Donna and I returned home for the summer, a new style of ranch management was in full operation. Mother and Jimmy were hiring one group of temporary hands after another to carry out all of the big jobs—shearing, putting up the hay, even trailing the bands to the mountains. Jimmy supervised the work performed by this series of ad hoc crews and handled troubles when they came up, but he stood now at some remove from the action, often unaccountably tentative in his role as overseer, spending less time working in the shed and corral than he did consulting—three or four times a day—with my mother on the porch. Gone was the hands-on authority, vigorous and decisive, my father had wielded as he directed every task. Gone was the comforting mesh of personal relationships he had maintained with the people who worked for him, the easy camaraderie among men who knew and trusted each other, laboring side by side all day in the shed and the fields, smoking and wisecracking, savoring their after-supper leisure together in the long summer twilights.

I hung around the shed while the sheep were being sheared and went out to the alfalfa fields to watch the hay being mowed and stacked, but I mostly stayed out of the way. When Jimmy suggested that I might want to go along on the trek with the bands to the mountains, I found an excuse to stay home. Donna had gone off to spend the summer with the Bradleys, and Joleen was still too young to take her place as fellow prankster and riding companion. Through June and July, I moped around, sitting for hours with my rifle on the edge of gopher town or wandering listlessly along the banks of the river, where I daydreamed more than I fished. When Johnny Matchett, a childhood friend of my father's, invited me to stay at his cattle ranch during August, I brightened for the first time all summer and was almost happy with the excitement I foresaw in this extended visit. Johnny kept a stable of registered quarter horses; I had always wanted to take part in a real cattle drive.

As it turned out, I never rode any of Johnny's horses, even double, nor was I allowed to go along on either of the cattle drives the men made during my month at the Matchett ranch. On the few mornings of my stay there, I jumped up early and ran out to ask Johnny what was going on that day. When he related his plans—to move cattle, for instance—I volunteered to join the crew. I was a good rider, I assured him, and had had lots of herding experience; I would be able to pitch in and do a good day's work. But he always put me off with a nervous chuckle and a pat on the head. His wife, he explained, thought that his son and I were still a little young to go along with the men. Reserved and watchful, Mrs. Matchett was always hospitable and kind to me, but to my dismay she treated me in the same fiercely protective way she did her only child, a fragile boy of seven or so. And Johnny deferred to her judgment in such matters. Unlike my father, he saw me as a little boy.

Instead of hanging around the house, most days I struck out with my fishing gear for Dupuyer Creek, which ran across one edge of the Matchett property behind the barn. It was a hard stream to fish, with banks overgrown with chokecherry bushes and clustered willows. By the time I had pushed my way through the prickly brush to gain access to a promising hole along the side, my thoughts would already have wandered from the trout waiting there to the excitement I imagined I was missing on the cattle trail, and then, inevitably, I would begin to reminisce about past summer days on our own ranch. I was coming to understand clearly now what life without my father would be like. I was getting good at wiping both eyes with a single pass of my sleeve.

A couple of times that month, I tagged along with Johnny when he went into Dupuyer to get supplies at Emmett Sullivan's general store. Emmett had also grown up with my father and always greeted me warmly. Then he would introduce me to anyone who happened to be in the store as "Bill Morehead's boy." I would look up hopefully at the unfamiliar face for some sign, a word or two of recognition, perhaps even a story I hadn't heard about Dad and his time in this place. I longed to have these left-behind folks affirm our connection, but none of them ever did. "Oh," the stranger would say as he suspended his business for an instant to nod at me without much interest.

Cut Bank

My mother held firm to her decision to give up the ranch and move us into town. But when school started in the fall of 1949, she hadn't brought the yearlings down from the mountains or finalized the details of the sale of sheep and equipment to Kenny Pardue, Art's son. Once again, she had to make boarding arrangements for Donna and me in Cut Bank. This time we were rescued by our friends, Orville and Vi Thomas, who offered to take the two of us in for a month or so until Mother and Joleen could join us.

When my sister and I arrived at the Thomases' right after Labor Day, their youngest son, a teenager who had been born with Down syndrome, welcomed us with mauling bear hugs and kisses. I had known Vi and Orville almost all my life and I had heard my mother talk now and again about how well the two of them had "shouldered the cross" of their son's disability, steadying his coordination so he could feed himself and button his shirt, encouraging each stammered word of his simple discourse, applauding all his small successes. I myself had never taken close notice of Bobby before, but each day that September when I returned from school, I looked forward to the sight of him waiting for me in the front window, to the affectionate flurry he met me with as I came through the door. At the time, I didn't compare my own dejected state to his loneliness and isolation, far worse a plight in spite of his two loving parents, nor do I believe now that it was pity for his situation that made me feel better in his company. But as he lumbered through the house after me, as excited at my arrival as a friendly puppy, I found unexpected comfort in this new association. For whatever reason, when I was around him, I wasn't angry or sad.

In early October, when my mother was finally able to join us,

Family portrait, fall of 1949.
From left to right: Joleen, myself, Mother, Donna

she discovered that finding a place to live in town was not an easy matter. There were virtually no houses for rent in Cut Bank, so when the Slotsvijs mentioned a tiny half-duplex unit open down the street from them, she hurried over and signed the lease even though the apartment was scarcely big enough for the four of us. These were cramped quarters, to be sure, she told us, but Joleen could sleep with her in the single bedroom, while Donna and I bedded down in the living room on rollaways she would buy. Of all our old furniture, only my parents' bed and chest of drawers and one overstuffed chair reappeared in our new home. All the same, I was happy that the four of us would all be together again, and the location seemed to me as good as anyplace in town, since my old friends, the Dyrdahls and the Newmans, still lived on the same block.

Even in the bustle of settling into new quarters and getting reacquainted with the kids in the neighborhood, there were moments when the realization that we had left the ranch for good would break over me in a fresh wave of melancholy. While my mother was arranging the furniture, unpacking our clothes, and putting away the dishes, she also advertised to sell Dad's two boats, the only items left from the ranch. A couple of days later, I stood out in front while a man from Valier who'd made a good offer on the pair loaded the folding canvas canoe onto the back of his pickup and drove away towing Dad's mahogany boat. As I watched him disappear around the corner at the end of the street, I thought about all the trappings of my former life—the sheep, the horses and dogs, the cab-over truck, and the jeep. Almost everything that had been special from that time was gone now. And not just things, but the people too. When, I wondered, would I again see Jimmy or Ida, Charlie or Andy? Would I ever revisit the north range or the old Monroe place or ride a horse across the river and up to the little grave on the bluff above the ranch?

In the year Donna and I had been away from Cut Bank, the people of St. Margaret's Parish had managed to raise the money to build a schoolhouse, a solid brick structure with central heating and a real playground, large enough to accommodate the growing enrollment they optimistically predicted. But in the fall of 1949, there were still fewer than a hundred students, and with only three nuns to teach them, the eight grades were parceled out to these ladies in the old manner. All the same, adults in the parish were quick to point out to one another the decided improvement of a mere three grades taught in tandem. Once again, my sister and I sat near each other in the same classroom where a single nun, Sister Irmagildes, orchestrated the activities of more than two dozen sixth, seventh, and eighth graders.

Of all the teachers I have known burdened with the task of superintending children of different ages while juggling their multiple curricula, Sister Irmagildes was the only one up to the challenge. In the style of the other two nuns who staffed the school, she was starchy enough, a plain-faced, all-business woman of middle years. But unlike her fellow teachers, she embraced her teaching mission with a zeal that snagged even dawdlers and daydreamers like me and carried everyone along in its momentum. Gone were the tedious hours of solitary desk work, the raps from behind for whispering or nodding off. Wearing a thick-soled shoe to equalize her shorter right leg, Sister Irmagildes moved like a queen up and down the rows of her classroom, weaving an intricate narrative web from the outdated book of spelling words, building a mathematical pyramid that rested on a solid base of simple sums and peaked in algebraic equations. However dry the drill or exercise, her imagination could build of its homey materials an impressive cognitive edifice, broad beamed and many windowed, spacious enough to shelter us all. Although the most advanced eighth graders scratched their heads for an answer a dozen times a day, the youngest, the slowest of her charges never felt neglected or left out of the excitement she made of dull learning. For the first time in my life, I sat up straight and paid attention in school.

On the playground, the serious business was still marbles. Instead of picking an occasional fight during recess, I returned to my old passion. As I worked on my rusty shooting skills—first in matches with the boys my own age, soon with older, better players—I discovered that an early accident with a wringer washer had given me an edge that made me hard to beat. One day when I was four, my mother had left her old Maytag running while she went outside to pin up a few pieces of laundry. Alone on the porch, I had first stared at the white rubber rollers grinding against each other and finally, unable to resist their allure, had climbed up on a chair to tease my index finger between them far enough to be pulled in almost to the elbow. The machine's safety release had saved my arm, but the thumb dangled from my hand, ripped loose from the web that had secured it. Although the thumb was stitched back into place an hour later in town, this ordeal left it permanently rigid, and slightly askew. Now the crooked appendage allowed me to fire a marble with a single movement, a piston action of the whole stiffened digit, while other players had to rely on the less powerful release of the secondary joint to drive their shooters.

I carried my everyday marbles to school in the cloth sugar bags my mother saved for me, but I kept a few precious agate shooters separate in a Bull Durham tobacco sack, its yellow strings drawn tight. Every night, I spread my burgeoning collection out on the living room floor, sorting the day's winnings into piles graded by their quality and coloration, putting only the inferior marbles, those with air bubbles or chips or hairline cracks, back into the sack I would take to school the next morning. If an especially good shooter remained in the ring at the end of a turn, it would be called in exchange for one less valuable unless the owner remembered to call out a "stay." More zealous competitors liked to break other players' favorite shooters by bombing them with steelies. The loss of a good shooter could throw my game off for a week.

Morning and afternoon, we raced to the playground to get in a full game in the twenty minutes or so allotted to recess. We drew a deep-ridged circle in the dirt. Only dead hits jumped this barrier. Then we set out the playing rules for each new match, always leaving room for a friendly bit of persuasion during the competition. Every move had to be called before it was played. Spiking— shooting from the elevation of one hand on the other—was not allowed unless the player had announced his intention before another called out, "No spikes." Drops—bombing the ring from above, usually with steel balls removed from shaft bearings—were permitted, but only a novice entered a game without first calling out, among a list of proscriptions, "No steelies."

I slipped out from under the no steelie rule with a special glass orb, richly colored and slightly bigger than a golf ball, that I had taken off the leg of an old piano stool. Because it looked like a marble and could function like one, I called it during any game for drops, sometimes causing a flurry of alarm among the other players but seldom raising a serious challenge. Even when others did protest my use of this weapon, I could almost always bring them around by appealing to the solidly literal cast of mind we all shared. "It's a special marble, but it's still a marble," my argument began. Standing above the ring, I would aim the glass ball; striking its target dead center, it shattered my opponent's marble.

A couple of us from St. Margaret's became proficient enough in the marbles ring that we began to venture down to the public school playground in the afternoons, picking up easy games among fresh competition. At first, we were welcomed by the group of hard-core players there, but after we had won a disproportionate number of matches, they began to react to the hustle, calling us "micks" and "mackerel smackers," sometimes refusing altogether to let "those dirty Catholics" play. It was during this period of petty harassment that I pushed Lee Dyrdahl off his bike one day during a scuffle and half a playground of kids chased me along Main Street as far as the Masonic Lodge before catching me.

Two boys held me while a couple of others took turns hitting me in the stomach and snarling insults at me and my religion. The kid doing most of the punching was an older boy, skinny and small for his age, his face flushed with unwonted confidence from the cheering support of his fellows. I sensed that he knew we were at least evenly matched—some of the kids looking on were calling out for the boys holding me to let go so that the two of us could have a fair fight—but he continued his pounding until someone finally pulled him away. After this beating, I stopped going down to the public school playground. I already had sugar sacks full of their marbles.

On weekends, I left my marbles at home and hung out with the neighborhood gang in the horseshoe of rock formations above the Cut Bank River at the end of our street. This configuration of layered giant stones framed the river ravine in steeples and bridges and ledges, making a natural playground where children who lived nearby scampered and climbed and formed associations to lay territorial claims to perfect hiding places and makeshift clubhouses among the overhangs. It was in this stone arena that my friends and I were inducted one Saturday afternoon late in October into the most thrilling pastime of that year of middle childhood—the BB gun wars.

Six of us—the Newman brothers, Lee Dyrdahl and his sister, Donna and I—were walking toward home when we were set upon by a warlike tribe of boys, eight or nine of them, all with home-made Indian hammers, bows and arrows, and BB guns. We had spotted them earlier from the territory we had claimed as our own at the end of the ravine. Although we knew the ambush was only a game, unarmed and outnumbered as we were, we simply fled, running faster than we knew we could, the sting of BBs on our backs and legs making the dizzy terror we felt palpable. As soon as we reached safety on the street above, we gathered in a tight, excited circle to plan a counterattack. Armed with our own lever-action Red Ryders, we started down again, giggling and scurrying from one sheltered overhang to the next, quieting one another's excited laughter with "Shhh" and "Listen" as we neared the enemy camp. Our assailants were sprawled on a ledge near the ravine, still crowing over their victory. Instead of ambushing them, we lay in wait behind boulders near their camp, surprising them with a barrage of BBs when they emerged. The battle raged on in boisterous engagement and giddy skirmish through the late afternoon until an adult voice echoed down from the street above with the first call to dinner.

On and off all that fall, until ice made the rocks impassable, and again in the spring and through the summer, we waged our war games among stone arches and ledges and in the narrow paths that crisscrossed the dense ravine brush nearer the river. As other children got wind of this excitement and showed up at the end of the block with their weapons, the simple mayhem of our initial battles evolved into a complex recreation, with ground rules as detailed as those for basketball or marbles. "Time out" really meant time out, and an expanding list prescribed acceptable reasons for pauses in the hostilities—to reload or borrow ammunition, to dash home at the summons of one's mother, to go to the bathroom. No older boys were allowed to join either side of any contest. Aiming at the head was strictly forbidden, and if anyone yelled "GIVE," even if he had been caught in a sneak attack, his assailant could not shoot. And, of course, no one was to tell.

Surprising as I find it now, no adults ever expressed alarm or intervened to put an end to our wild sport. Perhaps they didn't know what we were up to down there among the rocks or, if they did suspect, still failed to fathom the reckless nature of our turbulent, hilarious games. I shake my head, remembering the risks we took. No question, we should have known better. But, all the same, I smile conspiratorially with the boy I was. And I am happy that we were not found out, chastised, and hustled along to tamer recreations. Other than a few welts on arms and legs and buttocks, always the favorite target, there were no injuries. I know now it was not malice or cruelty that unleashed our warrior instincts, drove our breakneck charges, our quixotic storms against one another, but rather a deeper, less cultivated impulse, if one perhaps more savage—the pure exhilaration, the thrilling release children can sometimes discover in daring, frenzied play.

Although I forgot myself in these boisterous games for whole days at a time and in the playground marbles matches, I was still mad enough at the world in my less absorbed moments to get into more than my share of hostile scuffles. On the basketball court, where I started on the second team that season, I was so quick to face off with other boys that Mr. Hendrix, the coach, often nodded me to the bench before my stint of play was up. After watching these unprovoked shoves and snarling challenges for a month without comment, he took me aside one day after practice. "You want to tell me what your problem is?" he demanded after the other players had disappeared into the locker room. "Why have you got such a chip on your shoulder?" I didn't answer him. I suppose I didn't understand myself, at least no better than he could guess, what was fueling the hostility that flared in me at every imagined slight or minor infraction from another boy, and in any case, I wasn't going to try to explain myself to a stranger. After we had stood in silence for a minute or two, he shook his head and shrugged. "You ought to join my boxing club," he sighed, "put those punching instincts of yours to better use."

After this talking to, I tried to keep a tighter rein on myself on the basketball court and I thought about the coach's suggestion. I'd forgotten all about boxing in the two years since Joe Henderson's twice-a-week sparring sessions in the Nadeaus' basement. Those days seemed a world away to me now. But my friend Robert Anderson was a member of the club that Mr. Hendrix had organized for the Catholic Youth Organization, and one afternoon I went along with him to practice and signed up to join the team. Since we were the two youngest members and about the same size, we always sparred in the training sessions and were listed to contend against each other in the only tournament scheduled for the season. In this event, the older members of our team would face the boys of the Indian club from Browning, combatants who tucked their long black braids inside their safety headgear when they entered the ring.

I bought a rubber mouthpiece for the occasion, and a pair of green boxing shorts with a white stripe on each side. Robert and I were the first match of the evening, opening the tournament with three one-minute rounds in which we knocked at each other with side-armed swings more often than we delivered the stiff left jabs we had been coached to deal out. I had lost some of my early agility in the weight I'd picked up in the last two years, and Robert was a good athlete, wiry and fast, but I managed to hold my own against him as I usually did in our sparring sessions, and we put on a good show for the crowd. Although he bloodied my nose, giving him the psychological win, the bout was ruled a draw.

After the decision had been announced and the two of us had gone in to change, Robert's father and his older brother, the star guard of the Cut Bank High School basketball team, came back to the locker room to congratulate us. The two older men shook my hand and patted me on the back; there was no question, they told me, that their boy had faced a worthy opponent. Then, in a happy, uninhibited display of family pride, they huddled around Robert, chanting the praises of their young warrior. After they had left and Robert had followed them back to their seats near the ring, I stood under the shower for a long time, not caring that I was missing most of the evening's best bouts. As the steaming water pounded down on me, I tried again without much success to wash away the despondency I still felt at going it alone.

Adjustments

I was not the only one of us struggling to adapt to a family life without its center. Donna surely experienced the same problems of disequilibrium that I did, but the two of us didn't talk much about how we missed Dad and our old life. Certainly we never shared our separate sorrows and feelings of emptiness with each other, and as the year passed, we spent less and less time together. Perhaps naturally enough, she came to prefer the company of the two or three friends her age she made at school. Now whenever she got the chance—almost always on weekends, sometimes even on school nights—she escaped the cramped duplex and stayed over at her girlfriends' or went along on outings with their families. Joleen, who had spent her first five years as the family pet, doted on and catered to by Ida and Jimmy as well as my parents, was quieter now than most six-year-olds, more babyish and clinging, quicker to cry than she should have been.

During the first year after my father's death, my mother had been too harried and preoccupied with the business of running the ranch to dwell on her sorrow and loneliness. With less now to occupy her time, lingering symptoms of a forestalled mourning surfaced in this quieter place. She began to suffer from headaches severe enough to be diagnosed as migraines. At night, she often saw my father standing in the doorway of her bedroom, his image fading when she called out or reached toward him. When she told the three of us about these apparitions the next morning, she would hesitantly ask if we too had "seen Dad." These eerie recitals caused my older sister and me some alarm; Donna would look up from her breakfast to shoot a worried glance at me across the table. Mother began to seek solace in frequent visits to Father Hieptas.

Attending Mass every morning, receiving communion, seemed to calm her. We all went to church a lot that fall.

During our first months together in town, we gathered most often in the tiny kitchen. After-church breakfasts became elaborate, almost ritualized meals that dragged on through entire weekend mornings and somehow made us all feel better. We ate things now that had rarely appeared on our table at the ranch. Town food—deep bowls of sliced bananas awash in pasteurized milk, raspberries coated with thick cream. I hadn't guessed how many brands of cereal there were: not just Shredded Wheat and cornflakes, but Rice Krispies and raisin bran, puffed oats and Cheerios as well. Mother cooked paper-thin slices of processed bacon just long enough for each strip to curl at its edges before we ate them, one after another, with the crepelike pancakes she now always had time to fuss with. Neat slices of white bread popped up automatically, stiffened and perfectly browned, from a new toaster, ready to be buttered and sprinkled with cinnamon and sugar.

In mid-December, we traveled to Washington to spend the holidays with my mother's two older sisters, and for these few days, surrounded by her family, she seemed almost happy again. The train itself, with a day and a night each way to explore its mysteries, was the whole of the adventure to me, more beguiling than Christmas, than the smiling aunts and uncles and cousins I could hardly remember who met us at the little station in Zillah. The waiter in the dining car smiled when he removed the shallow glass vessel from the place set for me on the white tablecloth. I had never had occasion to use a finger bowl before, and unaware of its more ceremonial function, had washed my hands to the wrist in it, blackening the water. In the upper berth later that night, I awoke to the hissing of steam and the voices on the platform at each station along the way, and waited before I dropped off to sleep again for the lurch and sway of the car, the hum of the diesel engine beginning its measured pull, slow at first, now gaining a droning momentum as we moved out into the darkness of the countryside.

After Christmas, when my father's estate was finally settled, my mother decided we could afford a new car, a fast-back Buick she picked out at Friedman's Motors. In the process of closing the deal, she struck up a friendship with Walter Friedman, whose wife had died several years before. She and Walter would have a cup of coffee together each time she took the car in for service, chat about their children, and share advice about how to manage alone. I didn't even realize that I'd had any expectations about this association until late in the spring when I saw Walter drive by in a new Buick with a woman I didn't know. There were streamers flying from the mirrors of the car and a "Just Married" sign on the back. In the middle of mowing Bill Stephenson's lawn, I stopped short. If Mr. Friedman had wanted a wife, I thought, why hadn't he married my mother? But later, walking home, I was puzzled by my own reaction. I could hardly believe that I had entertained the thought of a replacement for my father, even in the capacity of keeping my mother company.

Although the people my parents had known for years continued to invite Mother to join their gatherings, she often begged off. Being around these old friends of my father's must have reminded her too much of his absence. Instead, she got better acquainted with people at church and made new alliances with people in the neighborhood, like John and Tiny Meyer, who rented the other half of our duplex. John had met Tiny when he came to Montana from Kansas to work on the road crews in Glacier National Park, and after they married he'd taken over management of her family's ranch west of Browning. Now they lived in town during the week so their teenaged son, Jack, could go to school. Most weekday mornings, Tiny sat drinking coffee for an hour or so in our kitchen, and she often invited my mother to join her and John for an evening of cards.

It was at one of these neighborhood socials that my mother met George Meyer, John's brother, who had also come to Montana after the war to work in Glacier Park and later joined the crew on Tiny's ranch. A small man, he dressed in the familiar gabardine shirt, wool western pants, and boots that everyone wore in those days when they came into town. But he was quieter and less outgoing than the ranchers I had grown up around, my father and his friends—almost shy in spite of his quick smile, I thought the night my mother first brought him over from next door to meet my sisters and me. By spring, he was visiting his brother and sister-in-law next door almost every weekend, and he and my mother were spending more and more time together.

One night early in the summer when Mother returned from one of her evenings out with George, she asked the three of us if we could keep a secret. "Someone has asked me to marry him," she told us almost giddily, "but I can't tell you who just yet." Unlike Donna, who had been watching my mother's brightening mood with great interest and growing excitement and now guessed that the mystery suitor was, in fact, George, I wasn't moved much one way or the other by this revelation. He was a pleasant enough man, I thought, and Mother seemed happy when she was around him. If anything, I felt slightly relieved, released by this new attachment from having to worry about her state of mind.

The next Saturday morning, and on several other weekends after that, George came along when we drove over to the west side of the mountains to visit my grandparents and my Aunt Jean and Uncle Lee. With money from the estate, Mother had financed a small ranch for her parents' retirement home in the scenic Bitterroot Valley. Now while my sisters and I played with our cousins, Sharon and Gary, and tagged along with my grandfather as he went about his chores—growing a large garden, tending the little herd of Columbian sheep he was developing, planting a new stand of alfalfa—my mother and George looked around the Bitterroot for a place of their own. In July, just a week after they had located a 320-acre ranch where they planned to set up a small ewe and lamb operation, they were married in the little church in Stevensville.

After nearly two years of separations and makeshift arrangements, our family would finally be settled down all together in a real home. To sweeten the deal, the former owner of the new ranch had thrown in two mares, a small quarter horse named Ruby and a big American saddle horse we rechristened Temple. Like my sister, who was enthusiastic about the move, I looked forward to the prospect of riding my own horse again. Still, during our last days in Cut Bank, I felt detached from the energetic preparations my mother and George were making, and while they packed up our things and talked happily about their plans for a new life on the other side of the mountains, I grew less and less ready to leave the old one. I wanted to make a last trip at least out to the ranch to look around—to wander through the shed and on down along the river, to ride out to the north range one more time. I suppose I was longing for some kind of closure, time for a private parting, before going off for good. But when I suggested revisiting these sentimental landmarks, my mother hedged. This probably wouldn't be a good time to go out to the ranch, she said.

Although we didn't return to the ranch, we did visit the cemetery—"to say good-bye," my mother said—on the day we left Cut Bank. George waited in the car while the four of us walked toward the stone that marked my father's place under the earth. In the two years since Dad had died, I had been back to the grave only three times, and it seemed to me now that "good-bye" was not what I wanted to say. I chafed at the unfairness of leaving my father behind. When my mother said that each of us should say a silent prayer for Dad, Donna began to cry. I squeezed my eyes shut and tried to picture what my father would look like now, his head still resting on the little silk pillow, his hands carefully folded across the vest of the brown suit. But my mental vision refused to cooperate with any clear image. I was already beginning to forget that dear face. By the time my mother patted me on the shoulder and started back toward the car with Joleen, the two of them walking along briskly now, on their way as members of a new family, Donna was lagging a little behind them and I was crying too.

Minutes later, we were crossing the cement bridge over the river gorge at the edge of town, heading west toward the mountains. I looked back at the rocks where we'd waged our BB-gun wars, caught a glimpse of the lot where I'd played with the neighborhood kids, and I wondered when I would see these places or any of my friends again. As the car climbed the hill beyond the bridge, I moved forward in my seat, ticking off familiar markers, watching for the turnoff to the ranch long before we came to it. By the time we reached the place, I was staring again through a wet glaze, each blink blurring the picture I had waited to see. After the car had whizzed by, I continued to peer out the back window for as long as I could make out the fence posts, straining for a last good look at the road to my childhood.

On the familiar highway we now sped along, one landmark after another—the Y at Browning, the bridge over Two Medicine River at East Glacier—flew by outside the window, each one triggering a nostalgic surge, calling to memory some happy scene. Charlie Cree Medicine and his crew might be haying just up the road from this crossroads, I thought. Along this stretch, we'd herded the sheep for a mile or so on the way to Heart Butte. Here, we'd turned north for a Sunday of boating in the park. As we left the grasslands behind and began to climb Marias Pass at the southern boundary of the park, I stared, dry-eyed now, back at the distant north range. It looked immobile, frozen. I wanted all that I had left there to be frozen in time like the north range, nothing to change.

Although more than twenty years passed before I returned to the ranch, I had no problem finding the turnoff from the highway on my first trip back to Cut Bank with my wife and daughter. In the time between, the narrow mud track had been widened to a leveled county road. Along with the grazing lands that once stretched beyond the Canadian border, the sheep had vanished; most of the reservation land, divided into good-sized parcels, was strip-farmed by white owners now. At the edge of the old property, we crossed the river on a new cement bridge put up below the spot where the old cable span had been, and on the other side the sheep wagons and the horse-drawn rake and mower had made way for a combine, a rod-weeder, a tractor—the machinery of a modern farm. But the houses and all the outbuildings stood where they had always been, still painted in the gray and red scheme my father had picked out for them.

No one answered my knock on the porch door at the house, nor did anyone appear in the half-hour or so that the three of us wandered around, through the outbuildings, then up onto the hill, and finally down to walk along the river. Harnesses and bridles and rusty horseshoes, a hand grain swath and sheep shears still hung along the walls of the shed. The paint sprayer that my father had bought the second spring we lived here lay in a corner of the granary. Up on the hill, we found a rusty rake and a broken-down wagon; near them, an old mower and discarded corral panels leaned against each other. As I walked along with my wife and daughter, pointing out this relic and that, I recited again for the three-year-old episodes from the familiar tale of "Daddy When He Was a Little Boy." The stories of trailing flocks of sheep high into the mountains and mowing an alfalfa field where baby rabbits lived, of riding a horse named Lily across the river and up to the bluff on the other side all coalesced in my single wistful thought, the wish that I could drive once more through the old north gate and look out across an unfolding open range where a man and a boy had headed out together to tend camp.

Later, in Cut Bank, we cruised by the old school and the church, the duplex near the river and the Nadeaus' house, where the town's optometrist now both lived and saw his patients. On East Central, where my father had shopped for supplies, Stephenson's had long since closed its doors, but the bars once frequented by ranch hands and herders were still in business along with the cafe, remodeled by another owner as a bar, where Dad and Wilfred ordered their last lunch together. Finally, just before it was time to drive back across the mountains to our cabin at Swan Lake, we headed out to the cemetery.

Inside the gate, I turned right at the first narrow road and pulled the car over to the side. Less had changed here in the time between, I saw, than in the surrounding countryside or on the streets of Cut Bank. The population of the place had grown, of course; there were probably half again as many headstones, many lying flush with the grass, more for the convenience of the mower, I remarked to my wife as we made our way across the lawn between them, than for the living who might come here to visit.

As an adult, I have always been wary in my expression of emotion, inhibited and cautious with the words that issue from my heart, suspicious of tears. But when I reached the stone that I had come to see, with the letters D A D etched in Roman capitals above the name and his dates, I shook with the convulsive sobs of grief I thought I'd buried years before. For all my years of circumspection, standing at my father's grave that day I might as well have been ten again, as I choked and rocked and finally doubled over in the throes of reborn sorrow.

Twenty years later, I came back to the reservation once more, this time to show my teenaged son, my father's namesake, his father's home. A sign at the turnoff announced that the old entry tract to the ranch had been officially designated Pardue Road, some latter-day county commissioner's nod to my father's partner, I supposed. The surrounding land looked much the same as it had on my earlier visit—naked farm soil stretching into the distance, not a sheep in sight. On the other side of the cement bridge, the old place was still recognizable even though the big shed had disappeared and a metal-sided machine shop had been added to the circle of buildings in the yard. No one lived in our former house now; the latest owners had put up a prefab structure for themselves in the place where the bunkhouse had been.

The young farmer, Dana Perry, was at home and invited us to look around. A friendly fellow, he walked along and reminisced with us. He had grown up here, too, had taken over a few years back when his father died. When I mentioned the little grave on the bluff, he remembered that as a child he had often wondered, like me, about its mysterious occupant. He pointed out a place on the wall of the granary I had forgotten, where my father's name and Jimmy's and Joleen's were scratched in the cement above the construction date. In the garage, now a storage place for junk, our old Monarch stove leaned against the wall, waiting, my wife laughed, for some recreational rancher to reclaim it as the antique center of his stylish kitchen. The buffalo skull that my sister and I had found fifty years earlier had been moved from above the woodshed door to a corral gate. When Dana offered me the trophy, I took it home.

We decided to stay overnight in Cut Bank, and after we checked into the motel there, I took my son to the ravine by the river and watched him scramble among the rocks, posed with him under an arch while my wife took pictures. With this new audience, I drove again past the landmarks of my childhood. The school was a senior center now and the cafe had gone out of business. I retold the old stories. We stopped to say hello to Ruth Bradley, an old family friend, and while we were sitting on her porch I saw Wilbur Werner, in his eighties but still practicing the law, walk down the street.

Late in the afternoon, the three of us drove out to the cemetery. Having missed the first right turn inside the gate, I drove us around in the maze of gravel paths long enough to admit finally that I had forgotten the exact spot and we might as well strike out on foot. Up and down uneven rows of graves the three of us made our way among the stones, my wife and son calling out to me, now and again, a name they recognized—Bradley, Dyrdahl, Stephenson. It was Will who finally found what we were looking for. The jolt at seeing his own name carved on the stone was still playing on his face when I caught up with him. This time, I was better prepared for the visceral firing the Roman capitals there set off, again, no simple tears but a loud, involuntary heaving of sorrow, which I rode out to its final mournful shudder.

That night after dinner, while Ann and Will stayed at the motel, and again in the morning before they were awake, I returned to the cemetery. I had never visited the grave alone, walked on it or kissed the stone. I paced impatiently back and forth around it now, talking angrily, to myself or to some ghostly third party, as if my father were a shadowy witness to my tirade.

Dad and I had been an unlucky pair, I told whoever was listening in, our time together cut short. He hadn't seen me—any of us—grow up, never knew what we became or shared in our successes. He never met my wife or smiled at the achievements of his grandchildren. Almost twenty years older now than he had lived to be, I didn't imagine that he was looking down on me. Instead, I thought about the brown suit, the rosary tucked under his hand, the shiny casket. How ironic that these things had stayed intact, even in my memory, while his body continued its slow transmutation into carbon, while his mind had being only in the minds of those he'd cared for. He and I had simply lost in one of life's great lotteries.

Leaving Montana

In the sheltered valley between the Bitterroot and the Sapphire ranges, the world felt smaller than it had east of the Continental Divide. Instead of miles of grass stretching to the horizon, land was tallied by the hundred acres here, mapped out neatly in fenced pasturage and fertile bottom land. A narrower sky faded earlier from day to twilight, slipped more willingly to darkness. Through the contracted landscape, seasons moved more gently, from April's cloudy-blossomed files of apple trees to summer fields planted in mint and alfalfa and sugar beets, row-cropped plots of peas and beans and potatoes, by July a patchwork of greens. Through the lingering autumn, jet trails of morning fog traced snaking paths of little streams across the valley floor and hung in the groves of cottonwoods along the broader Bitterroot, flowing north beside the highway from Darby to its lower reaches above Lolo. Shielded by mountain walls from bitter cold and howling, blizzard-driving western winds, the winter valley wrapped around itself, became a Christmas card of snow and silence.

On the new ranch, where we could see the neighbors from the kitchen window, the first job was mending fences. Without confines, George pointed out, the sheep might wander out across the road, trail into an adjoining field to trample someone else's hay, or bloat on a stand of oats. These were troubles we hadn't worried about on the open reservation ranges. While the two of us worked together to secure the edges of the property, he reminisced about his early days in Kansas. There, farmers like his father had fenced their fields, once and for all, in native hedgewood, so gnarled and hard it never rotted, he said approvingly, and marked the boundaries of their land with hand-cut limestone posts that stood for generations. Once our own less durable barricades had been put in decent order, we became the sole guardians of the flock of five hundred ewes my mother bought. There were no herders here. My sister or I would be called on by turns to ride out and check the band's location. On horseback, I could reach any corner of this little spread in minutes.

As soon as we had settled in, George bought a Guernsey cow, some chickens, and a steer, and introduced me to a style of work I had no word for. He called it "doing chores." Every morning, every evening, we milked the cow and fed the chickens, pitched hay for the steer, bottle-fed skim milk to the dozen orphaned lambs we had by early spring. Each morning on my father's ranch had offered an absorbing job to be accomplished whole. Brought up in the broader rhythms of work synchronized through the year to natural cycles, I chafed at this unrelenting round of slavish little tasks that were indifferent to the day or season. And almost worse to me than the drudgery was the confinement. Except for a few hours in the middle of the day, we stayed close to home. We never drove up to the park or spent a week at Swan Lake. Even on Sundays, when we visited Aunt Jean, just half an hour away, or stopped by my grandparents' place up the road, we were always back by five o'clock to do chores.

Cribbed and restless and bored, I frowned at my shifted life and looked around for other irritations. George wasn't a difficult man, unkind or hard to work with, but his attitudes and habits were different enough from the ones I'd learned to make me bristle. The world was full of things out of one's control, he'd shrug, not just wind and weather, but whether a sick lamb lived or died or how much a sack of wool would bring at market time. After a man had done his duty, met his obligations, what could he do but bow to fate? Hard work cleansed the soul, he honestly believed, and substituting an easier way of doing things somehow offended his sense of worth. Work had always seemed a consuming, almost joyful process to me, unrelated to the call of duty; I had no patience now for empty pursuits of virtue. Watching him plod along from one task to the next, I decided he had a narrow sense of purpose, that he often missed the larger view of what we were about. He built half a dozen more lambing pens than we could use because he had the lumber. Where three nails would do the job, he hammered five. On winter mornings, when the little truck he'd bought (a Studebaker!) refused to start until the sun had risen high enough to warm the engine, I muttered at his dogged patience. My father wouldn't have countenanced this needless delay, I thought. He would have found the problem and fixed it at its first appearance, or gotten rid of the machine.

Once in a while, I'd rebel and break away from George's way of doing things. One day, he set me to the task of clearing manure from feeding stalls in the corral. I could load it onto the truck, he told me, then spread it across the alfalfa field. Since I still jumped at any job that allowed me to drive, I got started right away with the pitchfork he handed me. But after shoveling half the morning at what had begun to seem a mountain of dung, I thought of Mr. Johnson on the next ranch down. The week before, I'd seen him move manure into neat rows with the grading blade of his Ford tractor and load it with the hydraulic fork onto a spreader, which layered it evenly over his fields. I put down the pitchfork and hurried over to the Johnsons'. When I drove up half an hour later in the borrowed tractor, George was more confused than angry that I'd left my post. He grudgingly allowed that what I had in mind might work as well and climbed up on the borrowed rig to show me how to run the loader. But when the corrals were clean in record time, the manure spread, I remained sullen and smug, too uncharitable and self-satisfied with my small victory even to thank him for his help.

The truth is I would have been impossible to please in any case. I was uncompromising and difficult, ready to be rankled at every turn. Even a man I'd grown up around, someone who'd known my father well and shared his views, would have fared little better in my opinion then. Simply put, no other home could take the place of the one I'd lost, no other man could measure up to the father I'd adored. My mother stayed out of the way, let George and me work out the kinks in whatever uneasy relationship we might find together. And he continued to suffer my reprovals and my churlishness with the same good grace he brought to any difficulty for which he saw no help. He stayed amiable and fair and never hassled me. I can't remember half a dozen times when one of us persuaded the other he was wrong, but years later when I left his house, he had both my affection and my respect. We parted friends.

On Sundays, we went to church at St. Mary's Mission in Stevensville. Mass was still said there in the tiny one-room church rebuilt from hand-hewn logs under the direction of Father Anthony Ravalli almost a hundred years after the original mission building burned. Near the church, a prominent headstone inside an iron fence stood at the head of this missionary's grave, while a simple wooden sign in a nearby field pointed the way to "Indian Graves," the unmarked resting places of his flock. Other Indians I had never seen before, migrant workers from Mexico, attended church here now. These silent, sad-faced people kept mostly to themselves. Many of them lived in converted railroad cars nearby, and because St. Mary's had no facility to educate the parish youngsters, they, like my mother, sent their children to the Etna Public School, two miles up the highway from our place.

At Etna, where there were again four classes in each room, I suffocated. If I had often been a mediocre student in the past, now I was worse than indifferent. The sole accomplishment of my seventh-grade year was a two-shelved bookcase I cobbled together in manual arts class as a Christmas present for my mother. Although my hostility had evolved into a more acceptable adolescent roguery that was winked at by most of the adults I knew and openly encouraged by my playground mates, the teacher was less tolerant. She determined early on that I was enough of a trouble-maker to be assigned the desk closest to her own. She was a big woman, overworked and unhappy in her post, who kept the windows tightly shut, no matter the season, and the thermostat set at 80. Wearing a dark blue wool dress, day in, day out, she gave off a musky effluvium of body odor and talcum powder. I held my breath for minutes at a time, buried my nose in the collar I'd dabbed that morning with George's Old Spice. I daydreamed and watched the clock, itchy for recess.

While I languished at school, my mother and George were facing up to economic realities. Through the winter, they watched with growing alarm as wool and lamb from Australia and New Zealand depressed the markets. By spring they admitted to each other that the boom years of the sheep business were probably over. Making a decent living from their small flock seemed a less certain prospect than it had a year before. When George's mother offered him the title to a Kansas farm she had inherited, they needed little convincing to accept. After three years of making business decisions, Mother wanted her new husband to take charge. George shrugged and allowed that it was probably for the best. There'd be no problem selling out in early summer, he said; the Bitterroot was becoming a popular recreational area, filling up with retired people who were looking for small spreads like ours to buy. On a Kansas farm like the one he'd been raised on, he'd know better what to do.

Montana, he still protested, was God's own country, but he was ready to go home.

Finally, summer came. In July I was old enough to sign up for the junior rodeo at the county fair at Stevensville. In the bareback steer-riding competition, my mount was a cream-colored, thousand-pound two-year-old Brown Swiss, whose skin hung loose across his back in deep folds. The nervous animal banged against the side panels in the holding chute as I lowered myself onto his back and gripped the surcingle wrapped behind his shoulders with my leather-gloved left hand. The object was to stay on long enough to reach a rope marker twenty-five feet away, but no one had told my steer the rules. When the door flew open, discharging us into the arena, he simply spun in place outside the chute, bucking slowly at first and then with more vigor, finally after half a dozen turns bounding forward toward the goal. By the time we jerked across the finish line, I was hanging from his side, my dismount a simple release of the cinch rope I'd somehow managed to grab with both hands along the way. I won two silver dollars.

In the tagging contest, an event akin to the catch-and-milk-the-wild-cow competition we'd watched at the Fourth of July rodeos in Browning, the challenge was to remove a tag from the tail of a four-month-old calf. The animal I stalked raced back and forth across the ring, fast enough to keep me at a distance. Finally, I cornered him at the far end of the arena, and as he bounced back off the fence, I grabbed for the tail. By the time the calf had regained his balance, slipped my grip, and bounced back into the open, I was holding the tag that would win me another silver dollar prize.

Ten days after the rodeo, we watched a loaded moving van pull away from the front gate, said good-bye to our grandparents, Aunt Jean and Uncle Lee and the cousins, and set out across the state again in the Buick. As we drove through Utah and on into Colorado, a high desert landscape I'd never seen passed by outside the window. I wondered whether any of the sheep in the huge flocks grazing on the grasslands near the highway had once been yearlings in the bands my father had shipped off from the station in Blackfoot. The hayers used tractors with hydraulic mowers here, I noticed, and new side-delivery cylinder rakes and wire bailers. Instead of rounded stacks like the ones Charlie Cree Medicine and his crew put up, neat cubes of hay dotted these late summer fields.

Perhaps to ease the melancholy we all felt, or perhaps, more simply, to pass the monotonous hours, George grew talkative as he drove along and told us about our new home a thousand miles away. The farm we would live on was near his older brother's place, the one they'd both grown up on, ten miles north of town. We'd put up corn and milo and alfalfa in the narrow bottom land there, and plant the contoured outer fields in wheat. The rolling countryside would remind us of the Montana plains, he said; buffalo grass had grown there too before farmers had plowed the ground a century before. Of course, there were no mountain streams and the creek beds were more often dry than not, but their banks were fringed in cottonwoods. The men wore bib overalls and flat-heeled lace-up work shoes instead of blue jeans and boots, and they cut the thumbs out of their work gloves so they could be reversed when the outer side wore thin. Talking about his old friends and his family, he smiled. We'd like the folks we'd get to know in Kansas—"salt of the earth," he called them, solid and trustworthy, good neighbors like the ones we'd left behind.

We broke the trip in Denver, stopping there for a day to wander along the crowded downtown streets, where I gawked at buildings taller than I'd ever seen. While my mother shopped with the girls at the Denver Dry Goods Company store, I walked up and down past rack after rack jammed with men's shirts and trousers like the ones my father always wore. Somehow I'd thought those western shirts, the canvas work pants and the gabardine dress trousers were uniquely his. Outside on the street again, a flickering image in the window of the store next door caught my eye. I stopped to stare at the tiny screen, amazed by the electronic marvel I'd heard about but never witnessed, and turned to say to anyone listening there, "That's television." It was 1951; I was thirteen years old. My sister's call reminded me that the others were already half a block away.

The next morning when we set out again, a searing south wind was blowing across the arid plains that extended east from Denver into Kansas. The road stretched out, straight to the horizon, dipping and rising now and then to hug the contours of the land. Nothing about the parched landscape it traversed reminded me of the rich grasslands at home. Where this road would lead me, what lay ahead, I didn't know, nor did the mystery of it stir me. We were simply moving on now, and I was resigned that a part of me at least would go along. For a while, the rear window framed the Colorado Rockies, a prospect hazier in the August heat than the view I'd looked west to see each morning on the ranch, but still a piece of that same spine of mountains that anchored my remembered world. When they had disappeared, I settled down into my corner of the backseat beside my sleeping sisters.

I'd left my childhood back there, I thought. Would my memories of it simply fade, like my image of Dad's face, as I traveled away from it into new places? No, I wouldn't forget. I could still call up all the sunny past days, play them out reel by reel, freeze one frame and then another for safekeeping in my heart. My sadness had begun to lift too, like the Montana sky in spring—overcast now and then but mostly clear, with whole days of whispy blue. School would be starting in a few weeks. I would meet other kids there, make new friends. In the meantime, as soon as we were settled in on the farm, there were things I needed to do. I would get a horse right away, I decided, and my temporary driver's permit so that I could drive again. I was taller now—once I put on a few more pounds, I would be almost full grown—and I felt like I could handle about anything.

Selected Bibliography

HISTORICAL SOCIETIES AND ARCHIVES

The largest holding of records, documents, and photographs in the state is housed at The Montana Historical Society in Helena. The University of Montana and Montana State University also have excellent collections of historical materials. Most counties support a local historical society. The Glacier Country Historical Society, Cut Bank, the Museum of the Plains Indian, Browning, and Glacier National Park, East Glacier, all have collections of material specific to Glacier Country, the Blackfeet Indian Reservation, and Glacier National Park.

HISTORIES AND ANTHOLOGIES

The best history of Montana is Michael P. Malone, Richard B. Roeder, and William L. Lang, *Montana: A History of Two Centuries*, 2d ed. (Seattle: University of Washington Press, 1993). John K. Howard, *Montana: High, Wide and Handsome* (Lincoln: University of Nebraska, 1983), provides a less formal but useful coverage of state history up to the 1940s. K. Ross Toole, *Montana: An Uncommon Land* (Norman: University of Oklahoma, 1959), details early development in the state, while *The Last Best Place: A Montana Anthology*, ed. William Kittredge and Annick Smith (Seattle: University of Washington Press, 1989), is a comprehensive anthology compiled for the centennial anniversary of the state.

NATURAL HISTORY, GEOLOGY, FLORA AND CLIMATE

A good source for the natural history of Glacier National Park and the surrounding area is David B. Rockwell, *Glacier National Park: A Natural History Guide* (Boston: Houghton Mifflin, 1995). Erik Molvar, *The Trail Guide to Glacier and Waterton Lakes National Parks* (Helena: Falcon Press, 1994) provides information about specific areas and the names of rivers, mountains, and regions in the park. A detailed yet easy to use geological reference for the area is David Alt and Donald W. Hyndman, *Roadside Geology of Montana* (Missoula: Mountain Press Publishing, 1986). The rich flora in the park and the short grasslands that extend east to the Dakotas are well documented in Per Axel Rydberg, *Flora of the Rocky Mountains and the Adjacent Plains* (New York: Hafner, 1969), and in James Stubbendieck, Stephen L. Hatch, and Charles Butterfield, *North American Range Plants*

(Lincoln: University of Nebraska Press, 1981). Beyond the daily reports and periodic summaries of the National Weather Bureau, Carolyn Cunningham, *Montana Weather* (Helena: Montana Magazine, 1982) gives a general description of Montana climate.

BLACKFEET INDIANS AND THE RESERVATION

Two excellent cultural histories of the Blackfeet Indians are John C. Ewers, *The Blackfeet: Raiders on the Northwestern Plains* (Norman: University of Oklahoma Press, 1958), and Percy Bullchild, *The Sun Came Down: The History of the World as My Blackfeet Elders Told It* (San Francisco: Harper and Row, 1985). A fine collection of historical photographs can be found in William E. Farr, *The Reservation Blackfeet, 1882–1945: A Photographic History of Cultural Survival* (Seattle: University of Washington Press, 1986). Like other Montana tribes, the Blackfeet were great storytellers. A selection of their stories along with a description of how they lived can be found in Hugh A. Dempsey, *The Amazing Death of Calf Shirt and Other Blackfeet Stories: Three Hundred Years of Blackfeet History* (Norman: University of Oklahoma Press, 1996), and George Bird Grinnell, *Blackfeet Lodge Tales: The Story of a Prairie People* (Lincoln: University of Nebraska Press, 1962). (See also *The Last Best Place*.) Two personal accounts of the Blackfeet culture can be found in James Williard Schultz, *Blackfeet and Buffalo. Memories of Life Among the Indians* (Norman: University of Oklahoma Press, 1962), and Clark Wissler, "The Sun Dance of the Blackfoot Indians" (American Museum of Natural History, *Anthropological Papers* 16 [1918]: 223–70).

SHEEP RANCHING

Except for the periods just after the turn of the century and during World War II, the sheep industry was small compared to those of cattle and swine. For that reason sheep ranching has not received the historical attention of those other agricultural enterprises. The following references offer an eclectic review of sheep ranching in the United States: John F. Bishop, "Beginnings of the Montana Sheep Industry" (*Montana* 1 [April], 1951); Jim Drummond, *Montana's Sheep Trails* (Helena: Montana Woolgrowers Association, 1983); Virginia Paul, *This Was Sheep Ranching: Yesterday and Today* (Seattle: Superior Publishing, 1976); C. J. Saterlie, *Here Comes the Wind* (New York: Comet Press Books, 1956); Edward Wentworth, *American Sheep Trails* (Ames: Iowa State College Press, 1948). A recent book by Alexander MacGregor, *Counting Sheep: From the Open Range to Agribusiness on the Columbia Plateau* (Seattle: University of Washington Press, 1989), details the important transition of a family's ranch from sheep raising to industrial agriculture and the effects on people and the environment. Two excellent memoirs on sheep ranching in Australia can be found in Joan Austin Palmer, *Memories of a Riverina Childhood* (Kensington: New South Wales University Press, 1993), and Jill Ker Conway, *The Road from Coorain* (New York: Alfred A. Knopf, 1989).

MONTANA PIONEERS

Many books describe the settling of the West, but few are specific to Montana or the important role of women. Both Otto Maerdian, *Pioneer Ranching in Central Montana* (Missoula: State University of Montana, 1930), and Granville Stuart, *Pioneering in Montana* (Lincoln: University of Nebraska, 1977) present histories of pioneers in Montana. A recently discovered manuscript on dryland farming in eastern Montana between 1900 and 1925 is summarized in Jonathan Rabin, *Badlands: An American Romance* (New York: Pantheon, 1996) and is now available as a memoir: Percy L. Wollaston, *Homesteading: A Montana Family Album* (New York: Lyons and Burford, 1997).

WOMEN AND CHILDREN

Women have received little attention beyond their political roles in suffrage and temperance work in the first half of this century, even less as equal partners in homesteading the West. Paula Evans Petrik, *No Step Backward: Women and Family on the Rocky Mountain Mining Frontier, Helena, Montana, 1865–1900* (Helena: Montana Historical Society Press, 1987), and Mary Ronan, *Frontier Women: The Story of Mary Ronan as Told to Margaret Ronan*, ed. H. G. Merriam (Missoula: University of Montana Press, 1973), offer histories of the roles women played in settling Montana. Emma Evers, "Life on a Montana Sheep Ranch" (*Montana Oral History Collection*, No. 50, University of Montana) describes her role on a sheep ranch in eastern Montana.

Children in the West have received even less coverage; only recently have historians developed interest in how their lives were affected by the sometimes harsh and primitive conditions of rural life prior to World War II. Two books address the lives of children in the new West: Emily Werner, *Pioneer Children on the Journey West* (Boulder: Westview Press, 1995), and the landmark work by Elliott West, *Growing Up with the Country: Childhood on the Far Western Frontier* (Albuquerque: University of New Mexico Press, 1989).

Among important sources on children and bereavement are Erna Furman, *A Child's Parent Dies: Studies in Childhood Bereavement* (New Haven: Yale University Press, 1974), Margaret Stroebe, Wolfgang Stroebe, and Robert O. Hansson, *Handbook of Bereavement: Theory, Research and Intervention* (Cambridge: Cambridge University Press, 1993), and William J. Worden, *Children and Grief: When a Parent Dies* (New York: Guilford Press, 1996).

MEMOIRS AND FICTION

The best-known memoirs on sheep ranching in Montana are Hugie Call, *Golden Fleece* (New York: Houghton Mifflin, 1942), and Ivan Doig's books *This House of Sky: Landscapes of the Western Mind* (New York: Harcourt, Brace and Jovanovich, 1978) and *Heart Earth* (New York: Atheneum, 1993). In addition, a clear sense of rural life in pre–World War II western Montana can be found in two novels by Hugie Call, *The Little Kingdom* (New York: Houghton Mifflin, 1964), and *The Shorn Lamb* (New York: Houghton Mifflin, 1969), and three historical novels by Ivan Doig: *English Creek* (New York: Atheneum, 1984), *Dancing at the Rascal Fair* (New York: Harper and Row, 1987), and *Ride With Me, Mariah Montana* (New York: Atheneum, 1990).